Hidden in the Cleft of the Rock:

A Woman Testifies

God bless you,

Show me Your Glory Lord

Susan J. Perry

by Susan J Perry

Susan J Perry
Edgewater, Florida

Simply This Publishing
CreateSpace Independent Publishing Platform

The Cleft of the Rock

Why do we run and hide?
Where can we go?
Go to the caves and stay hidden,
Or go for a ride,
So very far, far away.

Nothing can frighten you,
Or cause fear despite;
You are a child of heaven,
And you have every right;
To draw close to Him,
Our Lord and Savior;
He fights our battles first;
No rock, no cave can hide you,
Only the shadow of His wings.

Let's snuggle,
Let's see,
Where we are going?
No evil in sight,
We've resisted the devil,
And now he must flee.

Come to the mountain top,
Where the air is free and clear;
Go and join your beloved,
His voice to your ear;
Pray on bended knee,
And worship the King,
Sing a new song;
On high you will bring,
A melody so sweet,
Aroma to His nostrils,
And accept His holy ring…

The bride has found her bridegroom, atop the lofty mount,
Know He is smiling,
As your love doth surmount,
Any thing and everything the world has to offer,
Nothing better than the love of our Savior…

Psalm 61:1 Hear my cry, O God; attend unto my prayer.

2 From the end of the earth will I cry unto thee, when my heart is overwhelmed: lead me to the rock that is higher than I.

Song of Solomon 2:14 O my dove, that art in the clefts of the rock, in the secret places of the stairs, let me see thy countenance, let me hear thy voice; for sweet is thy voice, and thy countenance is comely.

DEDICATION

January 12, 2018

I am sure that today on my 66th birthday that God has given me the unction to open up the pages of this new book because many women are hidden in the cleft of the rocks all over the world. And just as Moses was hidden, we want to say to our Lord and Savior,

"We want to see your glory!"

We cry out to God and I know He hears us today! He will hear us tomorrow as He answers giving us the desires of our hearts. In today's world and as a Christian believer there is much that often goes unnoticed or swept under the rugs of homes and churches market places and everywhere you go they are hidden in the cleft of the rocks. God is calling you out of that cave! He is calling you out into the open for all to see. He won't allow them to throw stones to harm you or tip their hat in flirtation but because you are His, He has hidden you in the clefts of the rocks.

Hiding is definitely not a good thing. We cannot do this in God. He is to be glorified! We are to do this in every aspect of our lives and hiding will not produce good fruits. Well we are going to glorify God's name here in this book as women from all over plan and write about how God has been good to them. We are going to see and experience God's glory in these pages as God fulfills His mandate for my life and the lives of these women whom we are compiling these stories for.

Psalm 23:5 Thou preparest a table before me in the presence of mine enemies: thou anointest my head with oil; my cup runneth over.

God is so good because we will live out this scripture in Psalm 23 and our cups will run over with love for the Father, the Son and the Holy Spirit who causes all things to come together for His good. We are so blessed to dedicate this wonderful work to our God who is everything to us.

I know women need encouragement in this day and age and we are here to do that because God has called them, ordained them and set them free in these the last days. We have a heart after God as He says,

"Come out!"

He is calling you and you and you so hear His voice so your life will bless others. We are blessed to be a blessing: Your testimony will touch someone else who will touch another and so on and so on; God has a much bigger plan than we can fathom in our little finite minds and wills. God wants to bless you! God wants to run your cup over! God wants to use you! God wants to anoint you! God wants to see your face! Come out of the cave and stop hiding! He has taken care of your enemy. It is an honor and a privilege to serve our awesome God! There is no other! Many are hiding to find safety and you no longer need to do that, trust in Him! He is ALL that you need! Come and tell us your story and testify before others. God wants to reveal Himself to you in a deeper way.

LORD Jesus Christ, GOD the Father, HOLY Spirit we dedicate this book totally to you, every jot and tittle is yours. Thanks for all the help and inspiration you have given here. We love you eternally…

2 Corinthians 6:17 Wherefore come out from among them, and be ye separate, saith the Lord, and touch not the unclean thing; and I will receive you,

18 And will be a Father unto you, and ye shall be my sons and daughters, saith the Lord Almighty.

Thank You Lord!

SPECIAL THANKS TO ALL…

We give thanks to God for all of you because it is good to give thanks.

Psalm 92:1 A Psalm or Song for the Sabbath day. It is a good thing to give thanks unto the LORD, and to sing praises unto thy name, O most High:

2 To shew forth thy lovingkindness in the morning, and thy faithfulness every night,

3 Upon an instrument of ten strings, and upon the psaltery; upon the harp with a solemn sound.

Dr Frank and Evangelist Karen Sumrall: Thank you so much for all you do in and for the body of Christ, John and I love you so very much. You saw something in us that no one else ever did and ordained and charged us. You took us on willingly through the direction of our beautiful Holy Spirit and together we are building a lot here. As you go out to the nations and preach the good news of the gospel we continue to pray and believe with you. We support one another and raise up the name of Jesus together. Please go out and get the Sumrall's new book:

1) Glory Filled by Dr Frank and Karen Sumrall
2) Heart Throb Moments by Karen Sumrall
3) Faith is You by Dr Frank and Karen Sumrall.
   Please contact them on their website:
   www.sumrallministries.com

All are available on Amazon.com in paperback & Kindle edition

Psalm 2:7 I will declare the decree: the LORD hath said unto me, Thou art *my Son; this day have I begotten thee.*

8 Ask of me, and I shall give thee *the heathen* for *thine inheritance, and the uttermost parts of the earth* for *thy possession.*

9 Thou shalt break them with a rod of iron; thou shalt dash them in pieces like a potter's vessel.

10 Be wise now therefore, O ye kings: be instructed, ye judges of the earth.

Elsie Counterman: Thank you for your enthusiasm and zeal over our ministry and buying every book and for soaking it all in, literally; you are such a blessing to the Body of Christ. We love being your neighbors. Our lives are changed since we met you, thanks again our sweet friend. Elsie has a new book out as well:

The Way in Poetry by Elsie Counterman on Amazon.com

Psalm 95:1 O come, let us sing unto the LORD: let us make a joyful noise to the rock of our salvation.

2 Let us come before his presence with thanksgiving, and make a joyful noise unto him with psalms.

Bill and Connie Sparks: Thank you for being such very good friends and faithful and true pastors of the way, the truth and the life. How good is that? We love you and we love our fellowship together. You both are such a joy! We've been through some things together and God has always won the battle and brought us all to victory! God bless you abundantly!

John 10:10 The thief cometh not, but for to steal, and to kill, and to destroy: I am come that they might have life, and that they might have it more abundantly.

Sharon K Barr: A big thank you to Sharon for your generosity towards our ministry of books and authorship! You have been such a blessing and have supported our projects with your heart. Read Sharon's personal testimony in: A Stone's Throw Away: A Woman Testifies. (Available on Amazon.com) We loved working with her and the blessing in her. God bless you again and again my dear.

Deuteronomy 1:11 (The LORD God of your fathers make you a thousand times so many more as ye are, and bless you, as he hath promised you!)

John R Perry: God will glorify Himself through my wonderful husband, again and again! He has been such a blessing to me as he continues to pour into our books; correcting, formatting inputting these books into the publishing website, it takes him hours to work on these and I am so thankful for this opportunity to bless others with our talents. He will never bury his talents but lovingly puts these books in order for the readers to enjoy. Thank You Lord for the gift of my husband! Love you my dear, thanks so much! This should be my husband's scripture:

John 12:28 Father, glorify thy name. Then came there a voice from heaven, saying, I have both glorified it, and will glorify it again.

29 The people therefore, that stood by, and heard it, said that it thundered: others said, An angel spake to him.

FORWARD

Why the clefts of the rock you say? It seems like this is the hidden places where you can run in and find shelter during the attacks of the enemy; during those broken times when you cannot seem to face anyone else. Those times when you are hard pressed to find God much less be blessed by Him. Those dry times when it seems like everything you say and do dry up in you unto the very marrow of your bones. Who can find you during these times? You have only one source and only one resource and He is our God and He is all you need.

Let us define cleft: a fissure or split, especially one in rock or the ground; crevice, break, fracture or rent.

Women I have found out we are creatures who crave safety. Even in relationships they need to know they're safe in order for their hearts to give in and flourish. When I heard this, it made so much sense to me because that was exactly how I felt during times in my own life. The cleft of the rocks were a place of safety and hiding and women have this needy thing to be safe. It's okay and God is calling them out in this book, out into the Promised Land flowing with milk and honey where He will take care of every detail and not man.

Jeremiah 23:24 Can any hide himself in secret places that I shall not see him? saith the LORD. Do not I fill heaven and earth? saith the LORD.

Come out because your God has seen you. He has seen your hurt and betrayal; He has seen your pain and rejection and He is right there with you. He said in the Word that He would never leave you nor forsake you. Now forgive all and gently take the first steps out into the bright sunlight which will hurt your eyes at first, maybe be a little too bright but don't be afraid. Your God is with you and He will guide you back into all truth and love. Wasn't He the Shepherd Jesus Christ who went after the one leaving the 99 behind to fend for themselves? Get up, dust yourself off and be encouraged that someone needs to hear your testimony and many will read it, chew on it, ponder it and pray for you as well. Be strong and of a good courage as your waiting shall never be in vain but to the pure joy of the readers who already love what you have to say, can be a help to you. It's a great story; it's God-given, Savior-driven and Holy Spirit inspired so let's move on from here and get you started.

We ask each woman to tell her story in ten pages or less if possible typed into a Microsoft Word document attached to an e-mail to us along with a head shot photo in jpg format. We ask that they do include their favorite scriptures because our books are mainly about their experiences in Christ Jesus although that may not be a requirement any longer because God reminded us of the Book of Esther and although there is an underlying current, there is no mention of the Holy One. You just know that you know. But we would prefer it because scripture is truth and our lives often pattern after it. We would like to encourage writers to write and maybe get a jumpstart on their own books some day as they feel confident and led that it can be done. This book can be a new beginning for all of you. We hope that you will love it!

It's so funny today that as I remember being a young girl I had a penchant for rocks and collecting them. We lived alongside of a railway track that was later shut down because no one used it much. But I used to walk parallel with the tracks down a woody pathway and picked up rocks that caught my eye, which I was discovering. I was kind of a loner. Or it would be me and my brother Bobby who was a year younger than me. But I loved to walk and discover new shapes, sizes and colors of rocks. I did collect them for a little while but lost interest later in my teens when new adventures came calling. I find it fascinating that my God would put me in remembrance of these occasions and now I have written these two books with women's testimonies with rocks attached to their titles:

1 A Stone's Throw Away: A Woman Testifies

2 Hidden In the Cleft of the Rock: A Woman Testifies

 I guess I still find rocks and stones fascinating. In the Old Testament they used them to make an altar unto God where they worshipped Him. How cool is that? Jacob used them for a pillow as he had the vision of the ladders from heaven to earth with angels ascending and descending. The Bible says the rocks will cry out if we do not praise our God and I believe it!

Luke 19:38 "Blessed is the king who comes in the name of the Lord!"

"Peace in heaven and glory in the highest!"

39 Some of the Pharisees in the crowd said to Jesus, "Teacher, rebuke your disciples!"

40 "I tell you," he replied, "if they keep quiet, the stones will cry out."

Let us praise the Lord today, right now because we shouldn't ever want the rocks to take our place:

"Hallelujah! Hallelujah! Hallelujah! Praise to our God and King!"

Today while reading and writing this book please know that you do not have to be hidden in any cave or rock because we are hidden in Christ Jesus who keeps us; fights for us; sustains us and gives us His peace always. The Bible says this:

Colossians 3:3 For ye are dead, and your life is hid with Christ in God.

The Lord has led me to pray for the women of this book and the women who will read and glean from this book. So let's enter in:

Dear Heavenly Father,

We come to you in the mighty name of Jesus;
We enter into your gates with thanksgiving and your courts with praise. Father we ask you to forgive all our sins as we forgive those who have sinned against us and let your will be done on earth as it is done in heaven.
Father we thank you that peace will settle upon all those that read this because the SAR Shalom of God is the Prince of Peace, our Lord and Savior; we turn ourselves over to you and receive the Throne of Grace upon our lives.

Father we ask you to save our families; our friends and loved ones; our cities; our states and our nations for generations to come. We ask that you draw them by Your Spirit as the Word of God states. We thank You Lord for all you have done in our lives. We pray this book will glorify your name in every woman's testimony and help others get healed and delivered. Thank you Lord for this opportunity, may the joy of the Lord be our strength every day as we pray and surrender to you oh mighty God. You are the One, the only one. Thank you that our needs are met according to your riches in glory in Christ Jesus and this book which is dedicated to You will enrich every life that it comes in contact with. Glory to Your holy name, Amen.

RELATED SCRIPTURES:

Exodus 33:22 And it shall come to pass, while my glory passeth by, that I will put thee in a clift of the rock, and will cover thee with my hand while I pass by:

Song of Solomon 2:14 O my dove, that art in the clefts of the rock, in the secret places of the stairs, let me see thy countenance, let me hear thy voice; for sweet is thy voice, and thy countenance is comely.

Isaiah 2:21 To go into the clefts of the rocks, and into the tops of the ragged rocks, for fear of the Lord, and for the glory of his majesty, when he ariseth to shake terribly the earth.

Jeremiah 49:16 Thy terribleness hath deceived thee, and the pride of thine heart, O thou that dwellest in the clefts of the rock, that holdest the height of the hill: though thou shouldest make thy nest as high as the eagle, I will bring thee down from thence, saith the Lord.

Obadiah 1:3 The pride of thine heart hath deceived thee, thou that dwellest in the clefts of the rock, whose habitation is high; that saith in his heart, Who shall bring me down to the ground?

Show us your glory Lord!

Table of Contents

Chapter 1: Kathleen Knoblock Finne   Page 19

Chapter 2: Evangelist Marty Rogers   Page 26

Chapter 3: Elsie Counterman   Page 42

Chapter 4: Tamatha Finch Huff   Page 52

Chapter 5: Pastor Natalie Merritt Langford   Page 62

Chapter 6: Pastor Patti Renee Webb   Page 69

Chapter 7: Joy Hamm   Page 78

God's Love Letter to Women   Page 85

Chapter 8: Brenda Crumbley   Page 88

Chapter 9: Carla Pleasants   Page 98

Chapter 10: Fallon Hale   Page 118

Chapter 11: Evangelist Cherry Delaney   Page 127

Chapter 12: Susan J Perry   Page 136

Jesus is the Only Way   Page 153

Author's Corner   Page 155

CHAPTER 1

KATHLEEN KNOBLOCK FINNE

My Biggest Miracle

Proverbs 3:5 Trust in the LORD with all your heart and lean not on your own understanding;

I have always been a woman of faith, believer in miracles. When I was 35 years old, my Mom, at 59, was diagnosed with lung cancer. She opted out of chemo and did radiation.

They told her to get her affairs in order. I will never forget when my sister and I (both believers), stood in front of the hospital where she was, on the streets of Brooklyn, believing and praying for a miracle for our Mom to have more time. We felt Jesus' presence, because when "two or more are in agreement, there He is also." My Mom got another 2 years, which was a miracle. We tried to make her time as pleasant as possible. She was able to spend some time with my children. We would have liked more time, but that was what God gave us and we were blessed.

Fast forward a few years, my girls are teenagers, I worked long days as a letter carrier. I could not stay up all night waiting for them to get home, so I went to God in prayer. I placed my girls in His hands and He got them through their teen years unharmed. He filled me with His peace and I didn't worry like most teen parents do – another miracle.

My daughter Nicole got married and had a beautiful little boy, the love of my life, Ethan. Everything seemed great. Both my girls were in college, doing well, until Nicole got Lyme Disease, which caused gout and was very painful. Needless to say they gave her pain killers, which was the thing back then. She became terribly addicted and was in and out of rehab and wanted to get sober. I was raising Ethan. We prayed and believed. She detoxed from the pills by being put on Suboxone, which is like methadone, but only for short term, which we didn't know. At this point between the Suboxone and now she was drinking. She estranged herself from me, her father, my daughter Dawn, my sister Karen and my Dad. She would not talk to any of us for 7 years. She even stopped seeing Ethan because of her addictions. Again, my sister Karen and I were in agreement, every night, to pray for Nicole's "chains to be broken." Nicole dealt with spiritual warfare since she was a small child. I would come in her room and pray away demons, black angels, and terrible visions. I battled demons for her. She was raised a Christian, but the devil had a hold on her. We prayed for her to be released finally from these demons.

One day, September of 2016, she called me. It had been 7 years, but I knew the demonic hold was gone. I felt it; another miracle. She wanted to come home to us in Florida. She still lived on Long Island, NY. She had a horrible boyfriend she wanted to leave. We said we would be there in a few days. She changed her mind; she wanted to try to work it out with her boyfriend. Again, she didn't talk to me for 3 months; then another call. She said she was detoxing off everything. She got deathly sick. I didn't know she was still drinking. She still wanted to come to Florida, but needed time. We set a date to move her here in May 2017. In between that time, she was getting sicker. Too weak to pack, I said I would come help her. But I needed a hip replacement first. I could not walk.

It was April 17, 2017 when I had my surgery, and I was in NY the next week. My poor Nicole was dying from Cirrhosis of the liver. It was the result of the mix of Suboxone and alcohol all those years. I had hundreds of people praying for a miracle healing or a transplant. I had chaplains coming to pray in the hospital. I never gave up faith; neither did she. I had the opportunity to make sure she was saved. Though she was backslidden, she still loved the Lord, knew he died for her sins and that she was going to heaven.

The pain got so bad she decided on Hospice. I was believing for both of us, for all of us, because most of us, at that point gave up. Not me. Not even when she took her last breath. I did not believe she had passed. How could God not answer my prayer? How could He take her from me?

The days ahead were a nightmare. I have never felt such pain in my entire life. I knew she was with our Lord, but how could I go on with a shattered heart. How could I go on without my Nicole? We all went through the motions: making plans, memorials, trying to deal, still questioning why. Until one day, my beautiful daughter Dawn said,

"Mom, we did get our miracle. Nicole was suffering for so long with her addictions, mental illness, depression, and anxiety, God took her so she didn't have to suffer anymore, and mainly He gave her back to us. After all those years of estrangement, she came back to us. She didn't have to die alone."

I sat with Nicole for her last days as did her sister. We prayed, we talked, we forgave, and we all made amends, even Ethan, who suffered for years because of Nicole's addictions. We all came together in the end, for her. We all loved her so. She was the sweetest person ever. The drugs and the devil changed her. But when she was in that hospital, in the last weeks of her life, we had our Nicole back. God gave us the biggest miracle by giving her back to us so we could all make amends. We know we will see her again someday. My miracle continues daily as God gives me strength to go on until that day – Thank you Lord; till we meet again Sweetheart.

Psalm 23

A Psalm of David

*1 The LORD is my shepherd;
I shall not want.*

*2 He makes me to lie down in green pastures;
He leads me beside the still waters.*

3 He restores my soul;
He leads me in the paths of righteousness
For His name's sake.

4 Yea, though I walk through the valley of the shadow of
death,
I will fear no evil;
For You are with me;
Your rod and Your staff, they comfort me.

5 You prepare a table before me in the presence of my
enemies;
You anoint my head with oil;
My cup runs over.

6 Surely goodness and mercy shall follow me
All the days of my life;
And I will dwell in the house of the LORD *Forever.*

Amen.

Contact info:

Kathleen Knoblock Finne
Port Orange, Florida

E-Mail: **kodwyer@live.com**

Facebook:
https://www.facebook.com/kathleen.odwyerknoblock

Isaiah 45:3
And I will give thee the treasures of darkness,
and hidden riches of secret places, that thou
mayest know that I, the Lord, which call thee by
thy name, am the God of Israel.

CHAPTER 2

EVANGELIST MARTY ROGERS

My Life…

Some say when we are anointed that our lives do not belong to us…

But I believe that the decisions, the choices we make determine who we are in this life. The choices we make, whether to serve God or live for this world, determines where we'll spend eternity! So really life is all about choices we make.

When I was a baby, a condition called thrush or thrash in Alabama, back then it went through my body. The doctors couldn't help me so my parents took me home to die. GOD had other plans, and my Great Grandmother and my Granny Dunkin began to pray, and God healed me. My life has been a concession filled with sickness and healing. Praise God! When I was eighteen, because of things I went through, I had a nervous breakdown. I tried to commit suicide and had to have eight shock treatments. For six weeks I didn't know my name...

BUT God brought me through. I could have died when I overdosed on pills, but my Granny Dunkin's prayers brought me through. I believe I'm still alive because of her prayers! So many people have prayed for me through the years; my parents and grand parents, Pastors and friends and I thank God for them all. There are vials in Heaven stored up with prayers prayed for us. Thank you Jesus!

When I was in my twenties I joined a gospel group and we were the Southern Echoes. And I was the lead singer for many years. Glynn and Faye Hall traveled and sang with me for years! In 1975 we went to a gospel sing in Plant City, Florida. The church was having a revival and we were hired to sing before the Evangelist came up to preach. When we sat down the preacher started to preach, he stopped in the middle of the sermon and said,

"There is a lady here who thinks she has cancer; it's a bad spot so I won't mention where it is, but God said if she will come up, HE will heal her."

Now child, I was about eight months pregnant, and I had a big sore in an awful position, so I was embarrassed to even show it to the doctor. I was so bashful back then. I got up and waddled down to that altar as fast as I could move, the man laid hands on me and I literally felt that big sore fall off my body! Praise GOD!! God healed me right there! It was a miracle!

When I was also in my twenties I was in my car going to mama's house, I had three baby girls in the car and we looked up in the sky and saw a beautiful white cloud and in the middle of it there was a beautiful pink cross! My babies said,

"Look mommy."

I didn't understand then, but it was God trying to get me to walk into my calling way back then. I always dreamed I was flying. I knew there was something I was sent here to do. I just didn't know what.

I was raised Church of God, but no one ever told me about the Covenant. No one took the time to tell me about the anointing power of God. I'm not blaming other people; I just wish someone would have taken the time back then to mentor me. I guess it was all about God's timing! I had to be ready to receive and walk in all God had to give me!

In the early eighties I had a dream…

It was more like a vision, it was so real. I saw myself drown in a near by lake. I saw the one killing me. Then I saw the ambulance come take my body. I saw the funeral and I saw them take me to the grave sight. The minute I saw them put the first shovel of dirt over the casket, my spirit followed this bright light out of this world. Now this was before I knew about the "bright light" theory. I looked around and I was in a huge room with doors all around. I saw a person in a brown monk suit with his back to me. When he turned I saw his face and it was a skeleton. He pointed his boney finger and told me to go inside the first door. I saw a television screen and there were faces of people who were screaming with the flames of hell all around them. I started screaming and praying and that skeleton walked in and said,

"You better pray." And it said it over and over! It was terrible!

I woke up and started praying. I felt the Holy Ghost, and I started living as good as I knew how to. It's just I didn't know how to. The "ground up glass" religion I had been trained to "see" the things that are not really in the Word of God had me thinking no matter what I did, I couldn't live up to people's standards!

For years I thought I was living right. I was healed of cancer twice. I went to the Willow Oak Church of God in the eighties, my Pastor, which is still my Pastor, is Wayne Massey. One Sunday morning he stopped preaching mid service and said,

"Sister Marty, stand up, the Lord said you have breast cancer, and if you'll come down to the altar, He said He will heal you."

Now in my purse I had a prescription to go into the hospital the next day, because they found a lump in my left breast! I hadn't even told my mama about it. So the Pastor had no way of knowing, but GOD knew!!! Praise God! HE healed me right then and there!!

Then in the late eighties during another Sunday morning service, Pastor Massey said,
"Sister Marty stand up, the Lord said for you to get out of the business you're in and go forth and do what He has called you to do!"

Now I had four kids and making a huge amount of money so I thought, well as soon as I get ahead I'll quit my job and go sing full time. DUMB move! I had to face some terrible things because of that decision. I went through a hell that I didn't really think I could make it through many years later, all because of disobedience!

Then on March 31, 1999, I had another vision like dream, just like the other one. I saw myself die and all the same details as the other vision. The same awful skeleton but this time when I started to pray he said,

"It's too late now, it's too late now," over and over!

I woke up and got on my knees and totally gave my life to God! I was truly Born Again; the old me died that day and I began this magnificent journey. That day was Easter and I watched a movie about the crucifixion of Christ and it felt as if I was feeling the pain. And really seeing for the first time what Jesus went through for us. It was as if it had been a story before that I really didn't understand! But oh, that day changed everything. I was introduced to the Lord Jesus Christ really for the first time. It wasn't about religion; it was about creating a new relationship with the Lord of Heaven and Earth!

I started getting lost in the Bible! I had read it through before but it was like a Charlie Brown cartoon when the grownups talked:

"Blah, blah, blah," because I didn't truly know the Author of the Book!

This time as I read it, it came alive to me, and every time I read it through, I would find new nuggets of wisdom that I never knew existed. I learned about the Covenant that God gave Noah; I learned about the Covenant He gave to Abraham, Isaac and Jacob. All through out the Bible there are Covenant promises and I found out as long as we live the life the Bible tells us to live, we are included in all the promises. I discovered that Testament means Covenant and Covenant means promises and we can be included in every promise in the Holy Book! Glory to God!

Everyday I got closer to the Lord. I had a mini stroke in 1997, and along with the shock treatments earlier, my memory was a mess. I would forget where I was going, where the gas gauge was while I was driving, I was like a little kid. BUT that turned out to be a good thing in the long run. When God spoke to me and told me to do something, I just simply did it. Like a child, I listened to His voice and the miracles are still happening because of it! I read in:

Mark 9:29 This kind can come forth by nothing but by prayer and fasting,

So I started fasting, I made fasting a part of my life. I still see results from fasting, miracles that I never dreamed possible.

In the messages that kept coming, and being interpreted, five different churches, four different states; one part of the message I said I would be preaching the gospel and traveling all over the world. The Lord said I would have more money than I ever dreamed possible, but the money would not matter, it would be used for ministry. NOW every time I need money, it comes in. I have lived on faith for a very long time and God has never let me down!

I kept on reading the Word and fasting for answers. I wanted God's wisdom. I wanted to know more, grow closer to Him and be able to hear Him every time He spoke to me. I prayed Lord please let me hear You when You whisper to me! Praise God!

You see the problem I had was I was told not to believe in women preachers, I thought I was called to sing and write songs! Then one day in 1999 the Lord told me to go to Nashville, Tennessee. My husband is one of the most caring men I have ever met, he has backed me and encouraged me every step of the way! Even in my condition back then I told him what I had to do, he said,

"Baby you do what you think you have to do."

So I took off and went to Nashville, I thought it was to meet with a record producer, but I didn't like him and he didn't like me; that was not what God intended. So when I left that man's office I went back to the motel and prayed. The next morning I started back to Florida and the Lord spoke to me and told me to stop at K-Mart, so I did. I went in and got a cassette player and some tapes, I had no idea why He wanted me to do it but I did.

I got back in the car and put in the tape in the machine and the Lord said to push record and play. I came to myself about 45 minutes later and I was on I-75 South, and have no memory how I got there. I pulled off at a rest area and pushed rewind on that recorder, and I heard my voice preaching. I knew it was my voice, but it was not my words. The Lord spoke through me for about 45 minutes without me being aware of what was going on! He said that is how you'll preach and He gave me the scripture:

Mark 13:11 But when they shall lead you, and deliver you up take no thought before hand what ye shall speak, neither do ye premeditate, but what shall be given you in that same hour, that speak ye for it is not ye that speaks but the Holy Ghost.

Glory to God! He also gave me:

Galatians 3:28-29 there is neither Jew nor Greek, bond nor free, there is neither bond nor free, there is neither male nor female: for ye all are one in Christ Jesus. And if ye be Christ's, then are ye Abraham's seed and heirs according to the promise.

So it's not about gender, it's about obedience! Just simply doing what God tells you to do and not question! God opened my eyes to my ministry that day. Because it's not ministry, it's His and I'm just a willing vessel. I remember my first revival. I studied for a couple of months; it was Hanceville, Alabama which is about a 12 hour ride. I traveled in a motor home with some friends of mine and I studied most of the way up there. I had notebooks filled with notes and I thought I was prepared. We got off and started in and there was a big garbage can by the front entrance, and the Lord told me to throw those notes away; I argued, He won; I thought, what have I done?

We went in and set up and started to sing. Child the Holy Ghost took over and I didn't have to preach that morning, we had ourselves a time! Then the night service came, same thing. That was such a glorious service; everyone felt the power of God! I had a prayer line for healing that night, and a lady came up for prayer. I touched her and I literally felt her pain. She was hurting in her stomach, I felt the pain and told her where she was hurting and then I lay hands on her and the Lord healed her. The Lord told me to tell that lady that He didn't care how many men she had been with, HE still loved her and she was one of His children. The lady just grabbed me and cried. She walked off and the Pastor whispered to me,

"She used to be a prostitute,"

That night was truly a revealing experience!

Finally on Tuesday night I got up to preach, the Holy Ghost took over and the anointing came out of my mouth! Praise God it was awesome. There was a Methodist preacher there that night, someone had told him about the services and he wanted to see what was going on. He told me that he saw the anointing flowing and for me to never stop. Glory to God!

We came home. The Lord gave me the name of my ministry. It is: Tag Team Ministries, Inc. He told me to get it incorporated, and I said I didn't know how. But He sent a friend with the forms I needed to get it done. I drove to Tallahassee; because I didn't want to wait on the mail. We were incorporated in about twenty minutes after I walked in the office! The next step God told me was to start a radio program, I said Lord I don't know how. But He did. So I picked up the phone book and looked up radio stations. I closed my eyes and pointed to a station. It was WTWB in Bartow, Florida. I picked up the phone and called them and I was on the radio the next Sunday morning. I was on there for three years. I went to Carpenter's Home Church in Lakeland to be on their radio station and I was on there for three years, and on a station in Cullman, Alabama. I was on the radio until the stations went digital and I lost my technical partner and I haven't taken the time to get back on, but as soon as I can I'm going back on the air. I know God is going to send me the right people at just the right time!

My Granny Dunkin's brother, Homer Hackney was one of my first partners. We had a bond that I will never forget. I would write him a letter asking him questions and sometimes the answers would already come in the mail before I mailed the letters. There are supernatural things happening all around us right now. We just have to walk close enough to the Lord to receive all HE is trying to give! We started having church in my cousin's living room, we out grew that, and then we went to a store front. Then we went to a church, and then we had to get a bigger church. In the long run we wound up in the church where I had my first revival! I had the church in Alabama for five years, and the Holy Ghost moved in every service. I was the overseer because I live in Florida. My cousin pastored the church, it was a remarkable experience, but I don't think I will do anything else now but evangelize. I do love the Internet ministry and I want to go back on the radio.

One night on Facebook I was telling about the prophecies that I would be traveling around the world, this was before I actually began traveling abroad. I said I didn't understand why I hadn't actually traveled around the world yet, because it had been so many years. The next morning when I got up and checked my Faccbook page, a pastor from Kenya, Africa said,

"Sister Marty you are traveling around the world we read you every day!"

Praise God! Not to long after that I told my readers that I started out in the ministry with Children's Ministry. It was just my little mama and me. We sometimes had to make two trips. We would drop a load of kids off at Willow Oak Church of God and then go get the rest of them. They called themselves the No Limit Soldiers for Jesus! Now not too long after I post this, I received a picture of some beautiful little children from Kenya and they held a sign that read: NO Limit Soldiers for Jesus, Kenya Division! That touched my heart!

We will never know how many people we have reached out to until we get to Heaven! I just pray that I am a blessing to others as long as I'm here! There have been so many blessings, but there have been many hurdles also. I had COPD and had to be on oxygen for ten years. I would take my oxygen tanks with me when I went on revivals. I would leave them in the car, and because I read in:

1 Corinthians 1:27 BUT God hath chosen the foolish things of the world to confound the wise, and GOD hath chosen the weak things of the world to confound the things which are mighty.

You also have to remember my mindset way back then, all I could focus on was getting closer to God, but I had chronic memory loss. I went to a Neurologist for a year and when I went in he said I had chronic memory loss and a year later, he said I had chronic memory loss.

Digging deeper and deeper in the Word of God solved that problem! God healed me of COPD and He has blessed me with being able to remember the Bible. After reading the Word through several times it came alive to me. I would see myself as the person I was reading about. I would be, in my mind, walking in the desert with the Israelites. I would be the character, and try to imagine what I would do if it had been me. I found one day that I could name all sixty-six books in order. Then next I found that I could quote scripture and verse to so many verses and that is a miracle since sometimes I forget what I'm doing. ☺ I can remember over a hundred and fifty verses; scripture and verse. But it's all the power of the Holy Ghost; I sure couldn't do it on my own! I praise GOD for His anointing He has placed inside of me, and for drawing it out just at the right moments!

In 2000 the Lord told me to buy a computer, which I thought was strange since I didn't know how to turn one on! I had been an Executive on my worldly jobs, so I always had a secretary. I was nominated for Who's Who of America twice, and for Female Executive of the Year once. I had all these plaques and awards; then I truly found Jesus and I didn't need the world to acknowledge me, I just wanted more and more of Him! So I bought the computer and a friend showed me how to use it. I remember sitting down in front of that computer and watching my fingers move so quickly that it really scared me a little. I mean I didn't know how to type and the words were flying on the pages as I looked up. I didn't have to watch my fingers; it was as if God just took over my mind and boom, a little while later the first chapter of my first book was finished for me to read. I have had two books published, the first was:

Why We Dare to Dream

And the second one was:

Getting Round to It

I have about eight more books written and two movies and more songs then I could ever remember. All because GOD called me to do a work, and now all I want to do is find the right people to help me finish my mission.

   There is not enough room in these pages to list all the healings, all the miracles and yes, all the hard times too. I have seen visions of Heaven and I have experienced episodes of things that I really didn't think I could make it through! I know now that all the things I went through; all things I am going through are my testimony. These testimonies will be used to show others that IF I can make it, being in the condition I was in, anyone can make it! It just takes getting closer to JESUS and holding on literally for dear life!

As of 8/29/18 Marty posted this on her Facebook page: Evangelist Marty Rogers
4 hrs ·

I want to testify for a minute tonight...I have been healed two times before this one of cancer...I have been healed of rheumatoid arthritis...I have been healed of COPD, after lugging an oxygen tank around for ten years....over and over GOD has healed me...spared my life...and I have studied HIS Word and waited patiently for directions on where to go next. I have traveled around the world, just as it was prophesied over and over again in my life, and it hasn't cost me a dime...I leave to go to Rome, Italy and on to Greece on October 15...and I know GOD is going to give me the strength to go. You see we can sit and live in self pity. Or we can count our blessings and just keep moving forward till God does call us Home! I'm sitting here with no hair. no right breath...(real talk) but I am full of the Holy Ghost and ready for whatever God has in store for me....I am still alive at this time because of all the prayers that have been prayed for me and if I thanked you all till the day God takes me Home, I could never thank you enough! I feel an excitement that I haven't felt in a long time...

Glory to God and I want to preach. The BIBLE cover to cover and speak boldly and unafraid till my time is up...When it's time; I pray I go from the pulpit on to glory!! Praise God!

Philippians 4:8

Finally, brothers and sisters, whatever is true, whatever is noble, whatever is right, whatever is pure, whatever is lovely, whatever is admirable—if anything is excellent or praiseworthy—think about such things.

Contact info:

Evangelist Marty Rogers
Plant City, Florida

E-Mail: **rogersttm@aol.com**

Facebook: **https://www.facebook.com/evangelist.rogers**

1 Corinthians 2:7
***But we speak the wisdom of God in a mystery,
even the hidden wisdom, which God ordained
before the world unto our glory:***

CHAPTER 3

ELSIE COUNTERMAN

I was miraculously healed of MS and an inoperable brain tumor…

February 18, 1993 on a Thursday night I attended a Benny Hinn healing ministries crusade in Philadelphia, Pennsylvania because I suffered approximately ten years with MS and just less than a year I'd been diagnosed also with a brain tumor. It was a cold night in February, minus 5 degrees according to the local thermometers, it was frigid. We ventured out any way. I was desperate to get my healing!

The Lord kept telling me "I am making new cells" and I for one believed Him. God had me praying for new cells in my private prayer time one year prior to be diagnosed. I had to get my healing. This word about what God said was repeated by Pastor Benny Hinn himself when they called me up to the platform to testify of God's healing power:

"God says, He is making new cells!"

It is always good to hear a confirmation of what you yourself have heard to continue the process of healing. God is so good.

Women's Easton Aglow Lighthouse reports it like this:

"Elsie continues to stand in awe of God's loving grace, and His sovereign working power in her life. There are no meaningful words through which she can express her humble gratitude to the Lord, Jesus, for His healing touch to her body. She almost died at birth, weighing only two pounds. Only the Lord knows what He equipped her with at the moment to endure and to glorify Him. Later in life, He delivered her of Multiple Sclerosis and healed her of a brain tumor. Through much pain and suffering from this debilitating disease, God's Word continually strengthened and uplifted her faith while comforting her soul: ' I will never leave you, nor forsake you.' (Hebrews 13:5) Today, she serves the Lord by interceding for others by giving hope to those that suffer spiritual torment, mental anguish, and physical pain. She also plays the flute in her church orchestra. Come and hear her testimony. Be strengthened

in your faith, and encouraged buy God's loving grace and
mercy." Saturday, January 15, 2000

This is a definition of Multiple Sclerosis according to an internet research to aid you the reader with a better understanding of this malady:

The immune system works as a defense in fighting diseases or infections. Multiple Sclerosis (MS) is an autoimmune disease. This means that the body's immune system attacks its own body parts, such as tissue or nerves, instead of protecting them as it should. We don't know why some people get MS and others don't, or why it starts in the immune system. The immune system triggers MS activity because it causes inflammation, or swelling, in the central nervous system (CNS).

I began to speak and testify everywhere I went and they would hear me and I have good memories and records especially of the Women's Aglow Meetings. I have kept the flyers remembering now as I pull out the navy blue folder that holds these records. I was a guest speaker at Stroudsburg Aglow Lighthouse:
"Be aglow and burning with the Spirit"
(Amp. - Romans 12:11); A Women-to-Women Interdenominational Christian Ministry.

Tuesday, August 6, 2002: Elsie Counterman

Lighthouse Aglow Outreach: El Shaddai Assembly of God
"The Healing Power of God"
Monday, September 9th, 2002: Speaker: Elsie Counterman

Isaiah 25:1 O Lord, you are my God. I will exalt you. I will praise your name. For you have done wonderful things.

As I recall these great memories now July 16, 2018, some 25 plus years ago, I realize what a great miracle that I received and God has maintained my healing. I am living a full life now in Edgewater, Florida serving God in the local Church of God here knowing that God can and will continue to do miracles in people's lives. I am one of them. I have maintained my healing for all these years.

Tom Volk/The Morning Call newspaper headlines read:

A walk on the charitable side

Friends, family of MS patients take a stroll to raise funds
(No date available)

Walkers put their best foot forward to raise money for MS. They had a choice of a four-mile or a 6 ½ mile route at Hugh Moore Canal Park in Easton during the annual Super Cities Walk for Multiple Sclerosis.

About ten paragraphs in the article from The Morning Call of Allentown, PA read like this:

Worship Warriors, a group of seven members of Bender's Mennonite Church of Pen Argyl, walked for the first time yesterday, they celebrated the healing work in MS patient Elsie Counterman and prayed for other friends with the disease.

One of the Worship Warriors said people handed her final donations for the walk on the way out of church yesterday morning.

According to the Hugh Moore walk coordinator Sue Stauffer, "A lot of teams were formed by those who know someone with MS."

After my healing much communication went on between me and my doctors and Benny Hinn Ministries to verify and record my miracle. We had to be sure it was all God.

Early history:

I was born in Philadelphia, Pennsylvania 2 ½ months early and I stayed in the hospital for 70 days afterwards. I was a very sickly child. My mother died when I was just 17 months old and my dad remarried.

I had an adopted brother Bill, 4 years younger than I. On May 8th, 1983 4 days after his birthday; he was riding a motorcycle and was killed. I thank God that 7 months before, I had led him to the Lord. So he is in heaven today.

At age 6, I was hit by 2 trucks when crossing the street and while I lived, they learned that I have no depth perception and have never been able to get a driver's license.

I graduated in 1963 from Central Bucks High School in Doylestown, Pennsylvania. I moved to the Poconos in 1966 and I got married to Willard "Butch" Counterman on June 5, 1966. I worked then in the blouse mill factories for the next 13 years.

In 1975 I accepted the Lord into my heart. I have been serving Jesus in many ways ever since. The Lord told me I had to stop playing my flute for the world and I had to quit the musician's union in December18, 1976 as he instructed. I had played all over the Poconos for 10 years. I loved to see the smiles on the people's faces because they were so happy. I really missed those people because we had become good friends and I enjoyed the blending sounds of the musical instruments together, but I obeyed. As of today I am still playing my flute for Jesus and it has been 63 years now. It has been an amazing journey.

In 1977 the doctors found out I had a congenital heart defect of the left bundle branch block. When I was taken to the hospital after passing out, and they said I would need a pacemaker. My blood pressure was 30/20 and I ended up staying in the hospital for 18 more days. And this had also happened in 1971 and everyone said I looked so bad but I wasn't saved yet. I died and came right back before they realized it.

In 1983 my pulse went to 260 skyrocketing high above normal and 2 months later it went up to 280. I went to Heaven twice when I died while I passed out in my home. I got to really look around heaven; the colors were extraordinary almost nothing like here on earth. You see flowers growing right up out of the grass and I never saw any dirt anywhere. It was so beautiful. When I came back I realized earth was so ugly compared to heaven. In 1991 I was so exhausted and I went to heaven again. In 1989 they had put in a pacemaker and that helped me so much, even today.

In 2004-2005 my husband's mother died and we came down to Florida. My dad was alone at this time and we decided to move down to help with him. This is how we ended up in Edgewater, Florida to be near my dad.

In 2011 my husband Butch passed after much sickness. It was a very difficult time for me. One day I felt as if my chest was made of cement. Some thing was so heavy in my chest. I sat down with the Lord and I heard him say:

"I can take you home or you can forgive and fulfill your destiny."

God showed me my heart and I believe He made my stony heart, flesh; healed and set free.

Ezekiel 36:26 A new heart also will I give you, and a new spirit will I put within you: and I will take away the stony heart out of your flesh, and I will give you an heart of flesh.

I chose to obey and begin to forgive all those who had hurt me. After my husband died I had several people try to take advantage of me. Being a widow is not easy and I fell prey to some of them but now it was time to forgive according to the Lord. So one by one I did and I began to feel so much better. Some of this hurt had come from my husband although he had passed; I still had to forgive him.

July of 2012 I got baptized again in the Indian River here in Edgewater. I felt I needed to get cleaned up again after all I had been through and it worked for me. My life was changed. I have been active in church and I play my flute just about wherever I go.

2014, I volunteered in the local hospitals and nursing homes in New Smyrna Beach, Florida. I had to work with the chaplain and he trained me to visit with the patients as a volunteer. I really enjoyed this time. I prayed for the patients if they wanted prayer and I also played their favorite tune on my flute which seemed to comfort them always. Some called it music therapy. This is how I met my future Pastor, Bishop William T White. He was in the hospital quite ill and I asked if I could pray with him and he agreed.

In this hospital where I volunteered they were always joking with me and they had such nicknames for me as "the flute lady" or "the church lady." Either one was fine with me. I did it all for Jesus.

December 13, 2016 I got my good friend Gucci, my dog. He was a rescued dog and he was 5 1/2 years old, a Brazilian Poodle. He was already well trained and we enjoy each other's company still today.

Fast forward to April 2018:

I have recently written many poems in this year of 2018 and I decided to publish a book of them titled: The Way In Poetry by Elsie Counterman available on Amazon.com. It has been a lot of work in prayer and hearing the Spirit of God lead me through each poem; each stanza and each word. I had to hear it first and then I wrote it. I found pertinent scripture to go with my thoughts for each poem and I give all glory to God as my gifts have been expanded as they did for Jabez, it has been happening for me. I look forward to much, much more.

1 Chronicles 4:9 Now Jabez was more honorable than his brothers, and his mother called his name Jabez, saying, "Because I bore him in pain."

10 And Jabez called on the God of Israel saying, "Oh, that You would bless me indeed, and enlarge my territory, that Your hand would be with me, and that You would keep me from evil, that I may not cause pain!" So God granted him what he requested.

Contact info:

Elsie Counterman
Edgewater, Florida

Facebook:
https://www.facebook.com/elsie.counterman.1

1 Corinthians 4:5
Therefore judge nothing before the time, until the
Lord come, who both will bring to light the
hidden things of darkness, and will make
manifest the counsels of the hearts: and then
shall every man have praise of God.

CHAPTER 4

TAMATHA FINCH HUFF

Curriculum Vitae:
The Course of One's Life

NORTH CAROLINA

1972 - 1976
Born September 3, 1972

Lived with mother and father until 1976
Mother: talented musician – disabled (which became her identity)
Father: Vietnam Veteran and welding mechanic – alcoholic (which became his identity)

1976 – 1984
Parents separated moved with mother to Raleigh to live with Maternal Grandparents
Grandfather: Devout Church of the Brethren member
Grandmother: Housewife

1980
Grandmother died and Grandfather became primary caretaker
Mother's income was as "church pianist: to mostly Southern Baptist – Occasional fill in for other denominations. These were the doctrines that impacted my upbringing which I now know to be teachings of tradition seasoned with a dash of doctrine.

1984 – 1985
Mother remarried and we moved to Fuquay Varina, NC

1985 – 1989
Grandfather died, moved to small rural farming area of Duncan; Mother divorced.

1988 – 1990
Fall 1988, junior year of high school; Pregnant in August
Did not tell anyone I was pregnant until February of 1989.
My mom had my personal belongings on the porch when I got home from school February 1, 1989 stating that I was no longer her child.
Married baby's father in February 3, 1989 after given the choice of marriage or abortion.

David Todd Sears Jr born May 1, 1989
Graduated from high school in 1990

1989 – 2001
Verbal and physical abuse increased
Married, miscarriage at 16 weeks in 1994
Second son born March 2, 1995, Tyler Jack Sears
Suicide Attempt in 1997
Marital affair between 1994 – 1999
Separation from husband in April of 2000
Began seeing and engaged to person I had been seeing
during first marriage
Married again May of 2001

2001
Lost custody of my two boys due to my decisions
Me, the only person to ever bathe them, tuck them in bed,
prepare their meals and clothes, help them with homework,
care for them and nurture them, being told that I was unfit,
and believing it; Now just every other weekend participant
in their lives.

2002
Father died at age 53 from cancer associated with Vietnam
War – Accepted Christ just prior to death.

2004 – 2010
Sexual abuse in second marriage began and increased
Divorced 2010

1998 – 2010
Eating disorder – Bulimia

2010
Met final (and world's best) husband:
J Matthew Huff

2012
Married Matt
Bonus mom to 2 girls – Madison & Savannah
TENNESSEE

2011
Moved from Holly Springs, NC to Johnson City, TN
Began to experience life as a small fish in a big pond –
Living outside of the bubble
Matt and I traveled with his parents from Mexico – Canada.
We were on the road for 4 weeks. Eye opening that there
was more than what I knew or simply saw on TV.

ARIZONA

2012
Moved from Johnson City, TN to Ajo, AZ
Began to experience life as a minority; Only a small
percentage in the area were Anglo

2013
Matt broke his neck altering the timeline for AZ; what was
to be a one-year temporary residence, became a 3-year
adventure

2015
Arrested in AZ for assault; this after detaining a teenager
by the belt for police custody (dismissed). Proving that
man's definition of justice, which should be respected, will
fail

TENNESSEE

2015 – 2016

Moved back to TN to be closer to Matt's oldest daughter; Madison (16 at the time) removed herself from public school to be home schooled and moved in with us.

FLORIDA
2016
Came to FL to escape winter as we lived full time in an RV; during transportation, our truck caught on fire leaving us to have RV towed to FL. While the RV was being towed, it was damaged. We were stranded in FL for several months awaiting repairs. By this time, it was winter again and we opted to stay. And PRAISE GOD! This is where Matt and I encountered and yielded to the baptism of the Holy Spirit

2016 – 2017
Crystal River, FL

Fall 2017
Homosassa, FL
Forty-day testing: (Note: It was only after the fact that I learned it would be a total of 40 calendar days.) on September 1, 2017, just 2 days before my 45th birthday, God placed me on a journey. It was at Frontline prayer House and Revival Hub in Seneca, SC, here, God revealed that He desired that I attend a beautiful wedding. I had already accepted Christ, but now, it was time to prepare. To do so, He had to begin to scrub off layers and layers of dirt. This caused severe pain, rejection, unraveling (to the point of a second desired suicide attempt) and as the layers were removed, the more I wanted. It was evident that God desired fellowship in Eden, but that He was requiring I begin by staying with His Son in Gethsemane for one hour. I accepted the hour, knowing that our hour is not God's hour. He is still calling me deeper and it's possible since

October of 2017, only one second has passed in that hour. The journey beginning in September 2017 has taken me geographically to Mississippi, Virginia, Washington DC, North Carolina and then back to Mississippi. All to be lived out in Homosassa, Florida; all for such a time as this.

2018

In this moment, I live without regret, bitterness, shame, or guilt. In this moment, I live without a plan – simply knowing that God reveals every moment of every day. It's His 24 hours – he truly does direct my path. With that said, He is calling me to be in a place of purity before Him when He calls. At times, I am waiting on Him, but I'm standing in a mud puddle. He graciously beckons me out and waits for me to become weary of having to clean myself up; every, single time. I'm not describing works; I'm describing His constant faithfulness, and my constant wandering.

What you will not notice in this timeline, is the day-month-year, that I accepted Christ as my Savior. I don't know because I literally walked to the altar or prayed so many times. I don't regret not knowing the date, however how beautiful would it be to know when the angels rejoiced over me. What I do know, is that the physical and spiritual are congruent. The analogy of conception and child birth resonate with me. It's only when an ovum attaches itself to the womb, can a child receive the vital nutrients required for life. There is a period of growth required before birth. I attached myself to Jesus and He to me. I have only recently been birthed as a new creation in Christ and I continue to grow into His image. I no longer desire to live in His Permissive Will, but in His Perfect Will for my life.

INFLUENTIAL PASSAGES SO FAR...

Matthew 5:20 / 1 Peter 2:24
Jesus, the one and only Son of God atoned for my sins. He alone was the only sufficient lamb. No other blood, no other name, satisfied the debt.
Romans 8:1 / Luke 5:20
I am free

Numbers 23:19/
God can't lie

Luke 12:48b / Joel 2:25 / Mark 5:20/
2 Corinthians 5-6:2
I have been given much – I have wasted much – Much has been restored

2 Corinthians 10:5
Don't pretend to know more than God. Take all thoughts captive that do not glorify God.

Proverbs 4:23 / 1 Thessalonians 5:21 /
Matthew 18:15 – 18
Whatever is in my heart will guide my thoughts, speech and actions.
Unresolved conflicts won't go away. Humility (dare I say humiliation) is necessary to develop a servant's heart.

Zechariah 4:6 / Galatians 3:3-5
I can't do anything. And when I try, and strive, I will fail. It's only by His Spirit; The very Spirit that breathed life into me.

1 Corinthians 10:23
Everything may be permissible, but that doesn't mean its beneficial (soaking in this one currently)

Psalm 103
How can I be so vain as to think that it was my actions and decisions that led me to throw in the towel? It was God all along. He created me, called me, is healing me, revealing me, unraveling me; all for HIS Glory and eternal desire to be with ME.

1 Peter 2:23 / Psalm 18:2 / Romans 8:28 /Psalm 142
My only defender is God; My only provider is God. The only person who does not require words or actions is God. He reads, sees, examines, knows, feels, and understands my heart. I cry out to Him knowing that He hears – and responds in love and perfection. My husband, the one person on earth who knows me the best, can't even come close to meeting my needs. He was never meant to. I no longer set him up to be that person. Matt is my help-mate. God is soul's mate.

Philippians 3:14 / 1 Peter 3:15 / Romans 2:4
1 John 2:28 / Galatians 2:20 / James 2:1-4, 13
Am I loving well? Am I loving others, showing the same kindness and mercy God has and continues to show me? Am I pressing into Him/ Am I pressing upwards to Him or am I content with this level of our relationship? If asked, or not asked, am I ready willing and able to pour into other the overflow of God's love and character in my own life? Will it be a seamless transition from being at His feet now to remaining at His feet in eternity?

Genesis 1
I have only a beginning. I no longer have an ending. To live is Christ, to die is gain.

Contact info:

Tamatha Finch Huff
Homosassa, Florida

E-Mail:**TAMMYFHUFF@GMAIL.COM**

Facebook**: https://www.facebook.com/TammyFHuff**

Matthew 13:44
Again, the kingdom of heaven is like unto
treasure hid in a field; the which when a man
hath found, he hideth, and for joy thereof goeth
and selleth all that he hath, and buyeth that field.

CHAPTER 5

PASTOR NATALIE MERRITT LANGFORD

It was a difficult time…

I was in second grade when my mother decided to leave. She packed up her suitcase, took our family car, and headed out the door. My dad and I drew close during these times. We cried, grieved, and felt unloved. It was a difficult time learning to cope without my mom. My dad had to learn to cook, take care of a little girl (fixing hair, matching clothes, and private issues), and now provide means for that same little girl all alone. So thankful for family who gave us a motorcycle as a way of transportation; before the motorcycle, we hitch hiked a lot. On occasion, we would see what was once our family car, at the local tavern, which would only serve as a reminder of the past.

As the years went by, the visits from my mom became few and far between. She had moved on into a different life. My dad and I would attend church, where he would lead the choir and I would stay as close to him as possible. He taught me to sing and we would accept invites around the county to perform. I was brought up in church, knew the songs, knew the popular scriptures, received the gift of salvation, and was baptized; yet, so bitter towards my mother. Salvation, singing, memorizing scripture, etc. did not remove the past from my memory; the scars from my heart, nor the bitterness that had taken root. My dad was remarried when I was approximately 15. Oh how I couldn't stand this new relationship my dad had. I hated this woman with a passion; she took my dad's focus and time away from me. In my late teen years, I had developed my own life of busyness.

I was active in school, working a job, and had met a guy at church. Visits with my mom were once a year if that. I did invite her to my graduation ceremony but made sure not to give her a ticket to sit as part of the family, in order to avoid conflict. April, a month before graduation, I was asked to marry the guy I had met at church. Of course, I accepted. He and I were hardly speaking to each other throughout the next month. Graduation was tough. It was hard to celebrate with my father being so upset with me, remember we were very close. He did come to the graduation, as did my mother, but you could cut the tension with a knife. No one was truly happy. A month after graduation I moved out of my father's house, still not speaking to each other. I shortly found that I was pregnant. My fiancé and I decided to go ahead and get married. The next 2 months were emotional. I was scared of the future, missing my dad, and feeling completely alone, even though I was attending church and now involved in youth ministry. I ended up sending my dad flowers and asking him to meet for lunch. What a horrible experience that was. I had to tell him his little girl was married. I had robbed him of the joy of walking his only flesh and blood daughter down the aisle. He was so upset and hurt. I didn't dare tell him I was pregnant. He would find that out months down the road.

During the next few months, my husband and I were heavily involved in church, youth pastoring. God was working in my heart and filling the void and empty places. Eventually my dad came to accept my husband and at the birth of his first granddaughter. Our relationship was eventually restored. I also apologized to my step-mom for torturing her and making her life miserable. We started over and began a new relationship. As I started truly giving my life over to be used by God, He was working all things out for my good. God was moving in my life. He was restoring everything that was broken, little by little. There was just one relationship that still needed work. Every now and then I would see my mother at a store and all the bitterness would rise up in me from the past. I would remember the hurt, the pain, and all the tears her actions caused. She would never ask about me or her grandkids. Every conversation was about her or her new life. It was like daggers to the heart.

My husband and I continued to be used in the kingdom as youth pastors for the next four years. Then came the calling to pastor. We became pastors of a church in Chiefland, FL where we still are today, 15 years later. Even though I was now a pastor's wife and pastoring beside my husband, I still had unresolved issues with my mother. It affected me as a mom, wife, daughter, and follower of Christ. I had walls put up because of this hurt, rejection and offense. I was bound in this area of my life. I continually asked God to help me but felt nothing. I would go back home to visit family and would pray that I wouldn't run into my mother. Well, guess what? Every single time I went back, guess who I would see?

MY MOTHER!

Same old story, she would talk only about herself and the child she recently had. I would leave the conversation crying and then calling my dad. Of course, that didn't help my dad any to hear me crying. It would just stir up that dormant fire in him as well. Years went by with this continuing irritation.

TILL ONE DAY!!!

My heart and mind were prepared to receive instruction. God spoke to my heart saying that I had not forgiven her and if I didn't forgive her that I would not be forgiven. I had to release her of her past. I had to free her from the prison I had put her in. just like I wanted my dad's forgiveness for getting married behind his back, I needed to forgive her. As I forgave, God started working. She let God back into her life. She started attending Bible Study and reading the Word. God was showing Himself to her. He then brought her back into my life. She apologized for the past, told me things that I needed to hear, and a relationship was restored. She now calls me up to ask about how things are going, she spends Christmas at our house; has spent

Easter with us and she schedules times with me to shop or hang out. She sends me flowers on my birthday, etc. We have cried together, laughed together, and have discussed God's Word together.

Don't give up! Allow God to restore the relationships in your life that are broken. If He can do it for me, He can do it for you. God is no respecter of persons.

Some pertinent scriptures:

Matthew 6:15 But if ye forgive not men their trespasses, neither will your Father forgive your trespasses.

1 Peter 5:7 Casting all your care upon him; for he careth for you.

Deuteronomy 30:3 That then the LORD thy God will turn thy captivity, and have compassion upon thee, and will return and gather thee from all the nations, whither the LORD thy God hath scattered thee.

Contact info:

Pastor Natalie Merritt Langford
Chiefland, Florida

One Way Church
1560 NW 19th Ave,
Chiefland, FL 32626

Facebook: **https://www.facebook.com/1waychurch**

E-Mail: **chieflandag@bellsouth.net**

Psalm 91:1 He that dwelleth in the secret place of the most High shall abide under the shadow of the Almighty.

CHAPTER 6

PASTOR PATTI RENEE WEBB

My Testimony…

I was born in Los Angeles, California during the Depression times. My parents married the day after they graduated from high school and had two children; a boy and then me. Work was hard to find so my dad went into the Navy and went to sea for 6 months. I guess my mother got lonely and found someone else so she took us to Ohio. She heard about a third or forth cousin that wanted to adopt a boy, since she couldn't have children. So my mom took my brother to them and they took my brother in as their own. However, they did not want a girl or more children at that time. So my mother put me in an orphanage in Pennsylvania. I do not know how old I was at the time but when I was four a man picked me up at the orphanage and took me to the people who adopted my brother. He took me to the porch with my little suitcase and rang the doorbell and left. I watched this person walk away and get into his car and drive off. I only remember his overcoat and hat from the back as he left. I am told that when the people answered the door I said,

"Can I live here or don't you want me either?"

My brother had Scarlet Fever at the time and the house was dark. The doctor said that he might not pull through because he had no desire to go on, because he missed his baby sister too much. When he saw me standing there he jumped up and was healed instantly. I was told later that this was the beginning of a healing ministry.

My years growing up were not pleasant ones. The mother who adopted us only wanted a boy and kept me because my dad wanted a little girl too and since I made my brother happy, she kept me. She dressed me nicely, fed me and appeared to others to be a great mom. I went to the Methodist Church every Sunday, but after a few weeks; one day I was in bed (crib) and she got tired of me asking for water so she took the pillow and, holding it on my face, tried to smother me. Later in life she told me, if my dad had not come home from work early that day, I wouldn't be here. God had His hand on me even though I did not know it then.

I am only adding the next information so you can see how hard I tried to please this new mother. Growing up I was Homecoming Football Queen, played first violin in the Youngstown Junior Symphony Orchestra and played piano for 12 years. I was head majorette of the Baton Corp in the high school band; I was Sesquicentennial Queen of our town in Hubbard, Ohio. I won 3 Prince of Peace contests, I had the lead in two school plays; I was a lifeguard on Lake Erie during a summer, but nothing pleased this woman. I have forgiven my mother and found out some things that happened to her that made her the way she was. I loved and do love her. She lived to be 100 and finally she said she was sorry and that she loved me when she was 98.

Always there was criticism that when I went to college I married "the Fonz." He was the critical one because critical was where I was comfortable. I never felt worthy to marry someone nicer, so I would quit dating the nice guys when they got serious. Three children later and after years of him cheating and after beating me up when he was drinking heavily, I divorced him. raising three children ages 4, 2, and a newborn was not easy but always the Lord was there to get me through even though I never knew him in those days. Those days were another book.

Skip through 3 more failed marriages. More hurts, more physical and mental abuse and then I met Jesus. Oh how life changes us. You begin to learn and see that He never leaves you nor forsakes you. You feel real love for the first time, you learn to trust and rely on Him because He never lets you down.

I was saved in 1971 in a small church called Missionaries of Life that met in a house in Miami, Florida. I was working for a gym giving 4 exercise classes a day and worked with a saved girl and an unsaved one. The saved one kept pestering us to go to her church and one day we decided to go just so she would stop bugging us all the time. When we got there, people were singing with a band and raising their hands and then during prayer they were speaking in some language, we didn't understand. So I told my friend that we should start sliding toward the door and get out of this weird place. But before we could do that the pastor said there are two people in here that are not saved. We were snagged. I went down front because the Holy Spirit was prompting me to do so. Not that I knew that at the time but I do know now. The pastor told me to hold out my left hand, palm up and then he put a piece of paper on top of that hand, and then told me to put my right hand out, palm down. He then explained that the bottom hand was me and the paper was sin and the top hand was God. He said that sin was blocking my prayers and when he pulled the paper out my two palms were together. That was because God was now hearing my prayers and I was able to talk to him freely. He would always be there for me. He was, and now I can see it. What a simple way to see salvation.

Then comes the morning when you wake up and wonder what you are laying on that is poking you in the breast. I sat up and felt all around the mattress for a lump or button that was poking me. I found no lump in the mattress but found one under the breast – and it was not freely moveable. (I was married to a doctor at one time for 10 years and worked for doctors) so I knew when it didn't move around that it was not a good sign. I remember sitting at my big picture window looking out at the grass, trees, flowers and white clouds against a beautiful blue sky and saying to God,

"Why didn't I ever take the time to see how beautiful you made this world?"

I had not taken time to stop and smell the roses and now was it too late? Was I to leave my now grown children and grandchildren and leave suddenly when I was opening my eyes to observe all that I had missed? I had taken care of my mom for 20 years and she was living with me now. I never understood why God took my father and left me to see after the woman who never wanted me. At 98 she apologized and said she loved me. God knows even when we don't.

I came through the mastectomy and never felt anger or sadness about losing a breast. I was no longer feeling like I was a loser, but realized that I was always a winner in God's eyes! I had 9 months of chemotherapy, lost all my hair and yet through it all I was happy to be alive to serve my Father.

Just 3 months after I finished chemotherapy, I had a massive heart attack. They tried to do the balloon but it caused a piece of plaque to break loose tearing an artery so I had to have emergency open heart surgery. I remember saying,

"Why God, I don't understand?" But He answered simply. "You will."

I wanted so much to see my youngest daughter's first child (she was pregnant) because I had been with all the other grandchildren. I can tell you that this grandchild is going to be 23 on January 2016 and her sister will be 18 soon after and I am still here. I have 4 children and 2 step daughters, 14 grandchildren and 8 great grandchildren. I also found 6 of my 8 brothers and sisters.

Yes, once again He brought me through. One night, at a Joy of the Lord Ministry meeting, I had gone down in the

Spirit, and I had a vision while out in the Spirit; Jesus came over to me and knelt down, putting his finger on my chest, moving his finger down the length of my chest. It opened and then he reached into his garment and brought out a new heart and placed it in my chest and ran his finger upward to seal it closed.

Two years ago I lost my son. It was the shock of my life. Just when you think nothing else can possibly happen to you, the worst happens. He wanted to go up North and live in the snow because he had lived in Rochester, New York for some time and loved winters. So off he went to Wisconsin. He drove until God said this is where I want you to go. It turned out to be Green Bay. He got the flu and because he was overweight he coughed so hard that his heart stopped. He had a massive heart attack in his sleep. I was living with him when he left for Wisconsin. And we had just taken a trip together never realizing it was our last time together. God knew. So when I got the word that he had died, I felt I could not do this. It was something no parent is ever prepared for; but as always God brought me through. I never would have believed I could survive this but here I am two years later still alive and still working for the Lord. He is always good and always comes through.

"Do you see, my child, how many people you can help? You can talk to adopted people because you have been there, talk to people who had unhappy childhoods; to women who have been physically and mentally abused by husbands; to people going through cancer; to people who have had a heart attack; to people facing surgery (heart surgery, cancer surgery), chemotherapy and even parents who have transgender or cross dressing children because they are all the same lie. You can comfort them, giving them hope and a future, giving them the love of Jesus. You

can do so much for me because you have been through it all." And so I have.

I worked in the streets with the homeless; worked in singles ministries; in children's ministries; in deliverance, and so much more. God uses the broken people. He uses the unloved and unwanted and gives them love and a promise:

Jeremiah 29:11"For I know the plans I have for you" says the Lord. "They are plans for good and not for disaster, to give you a future and a hope."

In those days, when you pray, I will listen. If you look for me wholeheartedly, you will find me. Don't miss your healing, your chance to really live and know more love and grace and forgiveness than you ever imagined possible.

Pastor Patti will be 82 years young in December 2018. Patti was ordained many years ago under the auspices of Charles and Frances Hunter by Jimmy Bishop.

Contact info:

Pastor Patti Renee Webb
Sanford, Florida

Facebook: **https://www.facebook.com/patti.renee.love**

Psalm 17:8 Keep me as the apple of the eye, hide me under the shadow of thy wings, 9 From the wicked that oppress me, from my deadly enemies, who compass me about.

CHAPTER 7

JOY HAMM

I am glad to say I know Him as my healer…

I can't tell you all the times God has healed me throughout my life. I can share a couple of testimonies with you though. My surviving in 1963 when born three months premature was a miracle in itself. When I was two my mother was on Thorazine for her nerves; she was sleeping and I found it somehow and thought it was candy. I ate enough that they weren't sure whether I would make it but my mom had people praying. Doctors were able to somehow pump my stomach to get it out of me. I had no issues from the pills.

I am glad to say I know Him as my healer. I will share with you about what happened to me in 2015.

I woke up with a severe headache feeling like I had a sinus infection possibly. Two weeks before I had been having pain from a toothache so I thought maybe it was the tooth and a sinus infection giving the headache and making me feel so rough. I called the clinic in the little town I lived in and got an appointment for a few hours later. The doctor checked me and said she thought they were the same issues as I did. She gave prescriptions for antibiotic and pain meds. She said my blood pressure was high to come back on Tuesday so she could check it again because this was not normal for me. If I got worse I was to go to the E.R.

I went home and went to bed after I took my medicine. I called my friend because it was Saturday and I was itching but for some reason I couldn't see if I had a rash. I was concerned because in December 2014 I almost died from an unknown allergic reaction that started out itchy. It turned out I was allergic to the antibiotics the doctor had prescribed. I quit taking them. I slept mostly that day. Sunday morning I woke up and everything was black. I thought the electricity must be out, it'll be back on soon. I kept wondering what time it was and thinking it must be early because the sun's not up yet. I have no clue how long I lay there in the dark. My house phone rang and I knew right away where the button was to answer it, so I felt around and pushed it. My friend that lives 2 ½ hours away had called. My friend said that she had been thinking about me all day and felt led to check on me. I asked her what time is it and she said it was around 5:30, I responded, good it'll be daylight soon.

She said, "What? It's evening time, are you okay?"

It was then that I asked her to call another friend that lives in town and ask her to come help me and call 911 because I couldn't see anything. Thankfully my friend that lived locally came and helped me get my stuff together and stayed until the EMTs arrived and got me ready to go to the hospital. Once I got to the hospital they began to run tests. They said that I needed a neurologist and they didn't have one so they needed to send me elsewhere.

The next day late in the day I was taken by ambulance to a different hospital. I had not been there long and some doctor was checking me and ordering a cat scan. He said I needed surgery right away. He was concerned because no surgery room was available but he said he would fight to get one. Before we got in the elevator after having the cat scan done, the doctor called the nurse and said I was to go straight to surgery.

After the surgical procedure I was told that there was a mass on my pituitary gland the size of a softball. Supposedly this is a rare situation because most people have symptoms for years with this issue; it doesn't usually show up out of nowhere. I had an MRI over several years that should have revealed something but there was nothing. The doctor said he couldn't promise any sight to return because it had been over 48 hours since it started. He even stated it would be a miracle if I did. I said that it was okay, I served God and he is a miracle worker. We went through that a few times and I finally told him it was alright I knew he deals with facts but I was dealing with the truth and God had this situation and me.

I'd love to tell you I was able to see completely as before but I won't lie. There were consults with other doctors and many exams. The consensus was I had to go to rehab for a month at least and I'd have to have someone with me 24/7.

After a few days I was transferred into rehab. When I left the hospital I was already showering on my own, dressing by myself and walking the hall alone. These were things I was not supposed to be able to do. When the guy came to pick me up he said he'd help me on the gurney.

"Nope, I'll walk," I responded. He loaded my things on the gurney instead.

The rehab center was asking where the patient was when he arrived and he pointed at me and the nurse at the admissions desk said that we don't get patients that can walk with what you're dealing with.

"It's considered a brain injury," she said

As I went through time there all I heard was how they didn't know what to do with me because I was so high functioning. That my friends is a God thing!

While in rehab I was able to minister to many. That alone made it worth it. I had gone to the hospital in March 22 and on March 31 I was at my front door alone with no need of a caregiver as they had predicted. Again God!

I have not received complete sight as before this yet but according to the doctors my left eye has no central vision and I have little to no peripheral vision on either side. They also say 88 percent of optic nerves were basically crushed and there is no getting better, so I have to get used to not driving. That's their report. Mine is I'm healed and whole and my body functions as it was created to in the name of Jesus.

The neuro ophthalmologist said it would never improve. Last year when doing my check up he said that he didn't understand but was a slight improvement; I understand prayer and believing God at His word which works. I'm still believing for total healing to manifest physically.

I'm thankful during this time I was able to shine the light of Christ and I believe those I was allowed the privilege to minister to will never forget what God has done. What a wonderful thing knowing part of our salvation is healing. Thank You Jesus for opening the way and preparing us and giving your spirit to help us glorify you here on earth and receive from you in faith.

If you have a need just know He wants to meet your every need, you need only to ask.

My favorite scriptures:

Psalm 30:5 For His anger is but for a moment, His favor is for life; Weeping may endure for a night, But joy comes in the morning.

Jeremiah 30:17 For I will restore health to you And heal you of your wounds,' says the LORD, 'Because they called you an outcast saying:" This is Zion; No one seeks her." '

Mark 11:22 So Jesus answered and said to them, "Have faith in God.

23 For assuredly, I say to you, whoever says to this mountain, 'Be removed and be cast into the sea,' and does not doubt in his heart, but believes that those things he says will be done, he will have whatever he says.

24 Therefore I say to you, whatever things you ask when you pray, believe that you receive them, and you will have them.

Contact info:

Joy Hamm
Brooksville, Florida

E-Mail: **beautifully_redeemed@live.com**

Facebook: **https://www.facebook.com/tinksgr8aunt**

GOD'S LOVE LETTER TO WOMEN

When I created the heavens and the earth, I spoke them into being. When I created man, I formed him and breathed life into his nostrils. But you, woman, I fashioned after I breathed the breath of life into man because your nostrils are too delicate. I allowed a deep sleep to come over him so I could patiently and perfectly fashion you.

Man was put to sleep so that he could not interfere with the creativity. From one bone, I fashioned you. I chose the bone that protects man's life. I chose the rib, which protects his heart and lungs and supports him, as you are meant to do. Around this one bone, I shaped you....I modeled you. I created you perfectly and beautifully.

Your characteristics are as the rib, strong yet delicate and fragile. You provide protection for the most delicate organ in man, his heart. His heart is the center of his being; his lungs hold the breath of life. The rib cage will allow itself to be broken before it will allow damage to the heart.

Support man as the rib cage supports the body. You were not taken from his feet, to be under him, nor were you taken from his head, to be above him. You were taken from his side, to stand beside him and be held close to his side.

You are my perfect angel.....You are my beautiful little girl. You have grown to be a splendid woman of excellence, and my eyes fill when I see the virtues in your heart:

Your eyes......don't change them.

Your lips -- how lovely when they part in prayer.

Your nose, so perfect in form.

Your hands so gentle to touch.

   I've caressed your face in your deepest sleep. I've held your heart close to mine. Of all that lives and breathes, you are most like me.

   Adam walked with me in the cool of the day, yet he was lonely. He could not see me or touch me. So everything I wanted Adam to share and experience with me, I fashioned in you my holiness, my strength, my purity, my love, my protection and support.

You are special because you are an extension of me.

   Man represents my image, woman my emotions. Together, you represent the totality of God.

So man...treat woman well. Love her; respect her, for she is fragile.

May the Lord bless you and protect you.
May the Lord smile on you and be gracious to you.
May the Lord show you His favor and give you His peace today.
Numbers 6:24-26

Author unknown

Psalm 143:9 Deliver me, O LORD, from mine enemies: I flee unto thee to hide me.

CHAPTER 8

BRENDA CRUMBLEY

God will meet us where our faith is…

God still heals; set's free and does miracles today but not always the way we think He should do it.

This is my testimony of how God brought healing to my brother's life: my name is Brenda and I am married to Lee

Crumbley for about 1 year at this time. We currently have 4 children now, 3 sons and a daughter. Our mom Margaret Hawkins's father had gone home to be with the Lord at this time also. In my family there are 3 brothers and 5 sisters.

My brother David had been going to a kidney doctor for over 2 years. And they finally told him that he would have to have another kidney. He would need a kidney transplant, so he needed to sign up and be put on a waiting list for a kidney. They said it could be up to five years or longer possibly and he needed to check with family members also because there might be a match among them. So he had kept it secret until this time because he didn't want mom worried but he felt like he had to tell her now. So he called mom and told her just what was going on and what the doctor had said. So out of 9 siblings, 4 were healthy enough to take the test and I was the last one mom called. When I hung up the phone I heard you're the one to give him the kidney on the inside of me. I told my husband Lee about what was said and what I heard and he knew what I was going to say before I said it.

He said, "Whatever you feel you're supposed to do honey, I'm here for you." We were both in agreement with the plan of God.

I didn't know how He was going to work things out I just know if He said it, He would provide. Lee and I were both working full time jobs when we laid it all on God to take care of everything. When God gives you His plan, you can't try to figure it out.

I did say "Lord I know we could pray for him and you could give him a miracle," and I heard this:

"I will meet him where his faith is."

You see we try to get things for people from God that their faith is not in and they get mad at God. That's why we should listen to where a person's faith is before we pray for them. So they do not get discouraged and you won't either. The devil would love to steal the word out of you if he could. Jesus looked for their faith many times in the Word of God and He would say,

"Let it be unto you."

We don't know where a person's heart is at that time but God does. During this time my brother David was living with a woman for a number of years and her name was Joy. That night when he went to sleep, he was awakened by a voice he thought and hoped was Joy. He sat up in the bed and said,

"Joy what did you say? Joy responded by saying, "What did you say? What are you talking about David, I didn't say anything? Why what is it? Well I just heard that Brenda is the one to give you the kidney;" still neither one of us had talked to each other yet during this time.

A few days later we met up and we waited for the doctor to come in with the results. It wasn't long before he came in and said,

"Well I've got some good news. Out of all of them Brenda is the match to your kidney. What's even better it's like a twin to your kidney, this is rare to happen. It means you will have a longer life expansion with her kidney than with one that is a cadaver kidney. That's one that will last about 10 years maybe; this one could last up to 15-25 years as long as you take care of yourself."

So then the doctor goes into all the side effects of the medicine. He will have to take care of the rest of his life which did not sound good in the natural. They needed for me to come back when David did, so they could run more tests. They all turned out good on me but by this time David had put it off for around a year. The last test we took the nurse looked at David and asked,

"Are you sure you're not on dialysis," after seeing his test results? He answered, "No."

He was working a full time job still. To look at him, you would not have guessed he was going through this at all. But by this time he was starting to retain water and Joy told him,

"David this is a God thing and we need to get this done. He has taken care of everything for you."

The doctor said that we must set up the surgery and we can't put it off any longer or he'd have to go on dialysis. The kidney is dropping too low in its function. I told him after the doctor left the room,

"David I'm not afraid and neither can you be." He said, "I'm afraid something might happen to you." And I said, "Nothing is going to happen to me, God wouldn't have told you that if He wasn't going to take care of us both. So let's get it done."

The doctor set the appointment for the surgery and it was on my birthday and he remembered and changed it to 2 weeks later, June 21, 2003. During this time David and Joy got married before the date of the surgery. We came back for the surgery and as we all got there, we prayed and I told David that the Lord said to tell him that this kidney will last him for the rest of his life on earth and that he would be on the lowest medication possible. They took us both back and got us ready. As soon as they took the kidney from me and started hooking it up the doctor said it started working for him. They told him this might not seem like a big thing but it was. There was a man who held the world's record for peeing the most urine and he held that record for 7 years. And now David took his place in the world book of records; praise God He is good.

During the recovery time I was out of work for 6 weeks and during that time our sister Barbara called me and said she wanted to be the one to give David the kidney but she didn't get to so she said I feel like I'm suppose to send you a check every week that you are off of work. How much was your paycheck? I told her $500.00 a week and she said okay, I will send it in the mail. I didn't even think of the financial side of it at the time but God did and He took care of us all the way around.

Three years or so later my brother called me and told me that his doctor said to him in his visit,

"David, I've been in this field of medicine for over 40 years and I have never had one of my patients be on the lowest dose of medicine as you are. That's amazing and unbelievable as you are."

All Glory to God.

God is faithful to meet us where we are in our faith walk. We are still both healthy and strong. God still continues to help people with this testimony. 2008 God used it to help Pastor Zona Hayes Morrow when she had a transplant for a kidney and she would say during her preaching,

"Thank You Lord for my miracle."

One night after service she had a lady come up and I just so happen to be close by when she said to her how can you say you got a miracle from God when you had surgery? I could see the hurt in her eyes and I spoke up and said,

"God meets you where your faith is at the time."

And that person left with nothing else to say. It was often used after that in her testimonies. Always remember not to limit God on how He will do something for you or someone else. Trust Him and only believe.

Some of my favorite scriptures:

Proverbs 3:5 Trust in the LORD with all thine heart; and lean not unto thine own understanding.

6 In all thy ways acknowledge him, and he shall direct thy paths.

Matthew 9:27 And when Jesus departed thence, two blind men followed him, crying, and saying, Thou son of David, have mercy on us.

28 And when he was come into the house, the blind men came to him: and Jesus saith unto them, Believe ye that I am able to do this? They said unto him, Yea, Lord.

29 Then touched he their eyes, saying, According to your faith be it unto you.

30 And their eyes were opened; and Jesus straitly charged them, saying, See that no man know it.

31 But they, when they were departed, spread abroad his fame in all that country.
32 As they went out, behold, they brought to him a dumb man possessed with a devil.

33 And when the devil was cast out, the dumb spake: and the multitudes marvelled, saying, It was never so seen in Israel.

34 But the Pharisees said, He casteth out devils through the prince of the devils.

35 And Jesus went about all the cities and villages, teaching in their synagogues, and preaching the gospel of the kingdom, and healing every sickness and every disease among the people.

36 But when he saw the multitudes, he was moved with compassion on them, because they fainted, and were scattered abroad, as sheep having no shepherd.

It is God's will for us to be healed:

Matthew 8:2 And, behold, there came a leper and worshipped him, saying, Lord, if thou wilt, thou canst make me clean.

3 And Jesus put forth his hand, and touched him, saying, I will; be thou clean. And immediately his leprosy was cleansed.

Matthew 8:17 That it might be fulfilled which was spoken by Esaias the prophet, saying, Himself took our infirmities, and bare our sicknesses.

1 Peter 2:23 Who, when he was reviled, reviled not again; when he suffered, he threatened not; but committed himself to him that judgeth righteously:

We are all at different levels of faith:

Matthew 5:10 Blessed are they which are persecuted for righteousness' sake: for theirs is the kingdom of heaven.

Matthew 5:13 Ye are the salt of the earth: but if the salt have lost his savour, wherewith shall it be salted? it is thenceforth good for nothing, but to be cast out, and to be trodden under foot of men.

Philippians 4:13 I can do all things through Christ which strengtheneth me.

Contact info:

Brenda Crumbley
McDonald, Tennessee

E-Mail: **brenda_crumbley@yahoo.com**

Facebook: **https://www.facebook.com/brenda.crumbley**

Psalm 32:7 You are my hiding place; You preserve me from trouble; You surround me with songs of deliverance. Selah.

CHAPTER 9

CARLA PLEASANTS

Olive's Mess-age:
Mental Hell-th

Olive Branch~Prologue

"What are you talking about, I don't think getting rid of this baby is the right choice to do. You're trying to tell me Dr. Jones that I shouldn't even try to have this child at all! Are you crazy? Why would I even do that?"

"Well Ms.Ware the cancer you have isn't good for either of you. You run a very high risk of you dying, the baby dying, or both of you dying; I wouldn't give either of you six months to live either way. I recommend you terminate this pregnancy now." Dr. Jones said.

"It's against everything I believe in, and I will not do it. I am having this baby. Whatever God's will is, that's what's going to happen. If God says differently, then I will leave it in his hands and we will see what happens. He is in control of this baby and this situation..."

Shiloh was a determined young lady when she brought that healthy red headed baby into the world, she was so happy she'd went against the odds, and decided to say no to her Doctor's advice. Boy could that baby cry, and with such determination. That baby's name was going to be Olive.

As that little red headed baby grew it spent a lot of time with Shiloh's parents. Good people, decent people; Simple people that grew a garden and canned their food. They lived in the country on top of a mountain, far from everything and everybody.

Shiloh's cancer had started when she was twelve years old. Cancer wasn't a strange happening in her family, as a child from a family of thirteen she was one of seven more to get it. All the siblings had passed from it, except for one of Shiloh's sisters. She still had her battles with it too.

The cancer was like twins between the two of them. When one would get a certain cancer it wasn't long before the other one would get it, or something like it. None of them ever had breast cancer though. Shiloh was a walking cancer stick, with a variety to tell about.

Both of Shiloh's parents were true Christians, her father taught Sunday school for sixty three years. Every night, before bed time he would gather everyone into the living room and read a verse from the old King James Bible, that he carried to church every Sunday; He always had everyone get down on their knees, to listen or pray, as he would pray every single night, after the bible reading.

Shiloh had another surgery coming up and of course Olive would spend time with her grandparents until Shiloh would come home. Olive loved it there on that mountain. Such a peaceful place; population here was around two hundred. Olive's memories here would go through life with her; A decent, safe place; good people with a good upbringing; Teaching her right and wrong. Olive was six years old one Sunday evening at church when she accepted Christ as her savior. A lot of people would disagree on how she found God. The local Church in the little country town had a Christian movie night.

Olive was sitting on the back pew watching wide eyed at the screen as the actors and actresses brought to life what was going to happen to humans after God's return to earth for the saved. The ones that chose to accept him as their savior would leave the earth for seven years while the ones that remained behind would go through terrible, terrible times.

In these times people would have a hard time getting food and water, the only way to buy food would be to have a special mark from the devil on your forehead, or on your right hand, the mark would be the number 666. The times we live in now will be a picnic to what the people will go through in this seven year period called the tribulation.

During the tribulation water will turn to blood, there will be no fresh drinking water, everything will be rancid and stink. Loved ones will be killed in front of you in unimaginable ways to get you to accept the mark of the beast, or rather the mark of the devil. Painful sores, and plagues will be on the entire earth. Terrible weather and earthquakes among many, many horrible things will happen.

Olive saw a lady get beheaded by a guillotine for not taking the mark of the beast; it upset her so much she ran crying down the isle towards the front of the church.

"What do I have to do? I don't want to go through that!"
she exclaimed crying, and out of breath.

The deacon of the church took her by the hand and led her to the side room nursery and calmed her down.

"Honey its ok, stop crying and I'll tell you what to do and you'll never have to see anything like that happen."
"Ok…" Olive said with trembling lips.
"All you have to do is say Lord come into my heart and forgive me of my sins, can you repeat that for me?"
"Lord come into my heart and forgive me of my sins."
Olive repeated,
"Lord I believe you died on the cross for my sins and I want you in my life. I believe you arose on the third day."
The deacon smiled at Olive.
"Lord I believe and weakly smiled. you died on the cross for my sins and arose on the third day, and I want you in my life," she repeated.

*The deacon looked down at Olive, "You are safe now
Olive, no more to worry about."*
"Forever?" Olive asked.
*"Forever Olive, nothing can take you from God now, you
are his forever, the devil can't take you away or harm you.
When the bad things happen on this earth you will be gone
with God."*

Olive was so relieved and went back to the movies
without a care in the world, nothing she saw on the screen
bothered her anymore. The only thing she felt was sorrow
for the people who hadn't found God yet.

*"Olive, I know you just turned thirteen and your taste in
clothes are changing, but you can't wear jeans to church,
it's disrespectful."*
"But Mom..." Olive almost whined.
*"Olive, I've had my last say on it, Wednesday nights are
different, that's Bible Study. It's Sunday and you should
wear your best."*
*"Alright Mom." Olive sighed and went to her room pouting
but going to change anyways.*
*"That girl, I swear, she pushes me more and more." Shiloh
looked at Olive's Dad Charlie and weakly smiled.*
*"She'll be alright," Charlie smiled at his wife and squeezed
her arm as he walked by. "She's going through a lot right
now. Turning into a teenager, and getting ready to move to
a new state is going to be a big change for her."*
"Do you think she'll like it there?" Shiloh asked Charlie.
*"Yes, I think everything will be just fine. We will move
everything when school is out here in the summer, and
she'll have time to adjust to the new surroundings before
school starts in the fall. I found a nice church in the area
too." Charlie said.*

"Good, I'm scared and excited. This is all going to be so new and so different than anything we've ever done," Shiloh said.
"Well there's plenty of work out there in Virginia and we are only a couple of hours away from here so we can visit anytime we want," Charlie smiled at his wife.

Olive stared at the scenery as it flew by. She was riding in the moving truck with her dad and occasionally looked back to see how far behind her mom was in their family car. She was enjoying riding in the big moving truck, thinking it was kind of neat. The scenery was nice to look at, but that sadness wasn't leaving her heart and there was a knot in her stomach.

She was going to miss their house in the country. She was going to miss the mountains of West Virginia. She waved to old friends as the big truck lumbered past old school mates homes. She waved to her best friend Chelby and a tear formed, she would really miss her best friend. They had done everything together; sleepovers and school functions. As they passed the little town park she stared at the ball field and wondered what it would be like to go to a little league game there.

Olive was never allowed to go there and hang out with the other kids her age, her parents told her some of the rough kids hang out there and they didn't want her to fall into the wrong crowd. Sometimes her mom would let her go on the swings for a little while when she ran into the little hometown grocery store that was there, beside the park.

Olive's mom Shiloh kept her busy with all sorts of things. Olive thought about her mom and the things she did for her. Olive knew her mom was sick with different cancers but her mom always put on a smile and carried on strong for her sake. Olive looked toward the Rescue Squad building and remembered learning to march and twirl baton here. Chelby and she did that together too. They always had fun together. She was also going over a time spent there honoring her mother. It was a really big surprise to Olive one evening when her 6th grade teacher showed up at her house with the Rescue Squad people in tow.

It seems when Olive went to school one day, the teacher wanted the students to write an essay for a contest. The contest was for Mother of the Year Award. Olive had gotten in an argument with her mother that morning over something stupid. She couldn't remember what for, clothes or makeup, or something silly young girls and mom's argue about. Either way Olive did not feel like writing nice things about her mom. Why should she be Mother of the Year? All they did was fight over silly things. Olive would hardly consider that mother of the year stuff; she even considered writing about her best friend Chelby's mother instead. Olive remembered what her essay had said:

Mother of the Year

I think Mother of the Year should be Shiloh Ware. She is a very friendly person. She cloths and feeds me. All I need is her lovingkindness. The only time she is mad is when somebody does something she doesn't like. She washes our clothes. She feeds us. She plays games with us and goes places with us. She may work but she always has time for us. She puts up with me, that would probably be very hard. She's the best mom I could ever have. She even makes a fuss over me when report card time comes, good or bad. I'm the only kid she could have so she must feel pretty lucky.

Olive smiled to herself when she remembered how happy her mom was to win the award. Shiloh got to ride in the fire truck through the Mother's Day Parade with Mother of the Year written all over it. They also threw a Mother's Day breakfast, and had a bunch of people there at the rescue building. Small towns could be so fun. This little town was fifteen minutes away from where her grandparents lived. This little town of Mill Creek had a population of around seven hundred. Her grandparents town was about two hundred; it was called Valley Head. Olive was going to miss her small towns, where everyone knew everyone else.

Olive looked at the schools she had attended. She wondered what the new schools would be like. She played basketball here; she wondered what kind of sports they had at the new school. Maybe she would play basketball there. She had played piano for three years here; maybe she would keep doing that too. It was all so scary.

Olive sat higher in the seat as the moving truck entered the new town that was going to be their new home. The mountains had given way to rolling hills and eventually into the valley. The city had come into view and they were at the first stoplight. This would be different for sure; stoplights were not in the little town she was from. Not a single one; she looked at all the little businesses and thought how busy this place was going to be.

As they arrived at the other end of this new town Olive sat in the big moving truck and gasped in horror at where they were going to be moving into. A trailer and a little one at that! It seemed the trailer wasn't much bigger than the moving truck she was sitting in. she was already missing her big house in West Virginia even more.

Olive climbed down out of the truck and walked into the little place that was going to be their new home. As she walked down the little hall she felt like puking. Why couldn't they have just left her in West Virginia on that two hundred acre mountain, with her grandparents? The big six bedroom, three story house, would have had plenty of room for her in it.

Olive walked outside again to the big moving truck, and sat down in the seat and bust out bawling. Her mom walked over to her.

"Olive it's going to be okay. I know its small but we will look for a place in the country. There wasn't anything available yet in our price range, so we took what we could find for right now. God will take care of us, it's just a small bump in the road. Come back inside with me, they are going to set your bedroom up."

Olive stared in horror as they looked into what was going to be her bedroom. Apparently the room was so small her twin size bed wasn't going to fit inside the room! They were going to have to get a pull down blind to put at her doorway, because they couldn't shut the door as the twin size bed was too long. What was wrong with these people? She wanted her privacy.

She thought about her huge bedroom she'd grown accustomed to, oh she was going to miss it. That bedroom could hold two beds, two dressers, a big comfy chair, a desk and there had been a lot of leftover space with all that in there. Not so here.

They managed to cram everything into the small place. So many changes it was ridiculous. The big chest freezer sat in the hallway, outside Olive's room. Apparently this space would have been intended for a washer and dryer with normal people, but the landlord here didn't allow any washers and dryers; Laundromat ugh. Somehow they managed to squeeze Olive's piano into the tiny living room of this place. The rest of the stuff got squeezed in around it.

Olive's next crisis after that was the heat. It was June but it felt like a sauna in this tin can; no air conditioning. Apparently everything was supposed to be ok with the purchase of a mini blind for her bedroom doorway, and three oscillating fans. One fan for each bedroom and the living room. The mountains never would get hot like this, and never had she felt humidity like this, ugh.

The first night Olive sat, bolt up right in bed to a terrible thundering and clanging; what in the world was this terrible noise? She ran into the middle of the hall and grabbed onto the freezer. The whole trailer was shaking and vibrating. She stared wild-eyed at everything, trying to focus from being asleep. Her heart was pounding so hard, it felt like it was coming out of her chest.

"Whaaat is this awful noise and shaking?" she was asking, as her mom came out of her parent's room and took her arm for comfort. "Olive, it's the train. It's ok honey. Go back to bed it's only four in the morning. Go get some sleep."

Olive shuffled back to bed to keep her mom happy, but she was far from happy, and far from sleeping. She lay on top of the bed covers staring at her new surroundings, as sweat poured off of her from the heat. She lay there waiting for the rumbling and clanging to quit, and quiet to come again. The only other time she experienced any kind of thing this traumatic was a severe thunderstorm back home.

She had woke up in the night to a terrible thunderstorm, and just like tonight, her mom had comforted her and let her know it was going to be ok. Olive thought the two oak trees in her old yard would get struck by lightening or get blown over into their house during that storm. They didn't. That particular night she'd been calmed down enough by her mom, to go back to sleep, not this time.

Olive lay there thinking about the little dog they had to give to her grandparents. The landlady here didn't allow animals. I don't think she allowed much of anything. Hopefully time would go fast here in this tin can, and they could get the little dog back, when they got into the country. The dog had been in the family for ten years, and even though the dog had been attached to Shiloh more than anybody it was still their entire family's pet. That dog had always slept in Olive's room in a little basket at the foot of her bed.

The next month or so was very busy setting up the new living arrangements; running errands, enrolling in the new school, attending the new church. Shiloh got a part-time job working for a local company that helped handicapped people.

It was summer vacation still and Olive was very lost with what to do with herself. She wrote letters to old friends and mostly read books; bored mainly. People from back home were so friendly, everyone would wave at each other when they went by, whether they knew you or not. Here, everyone seemed rude, and tried to avoid each other. So Olive sunk deeper into sadness, depression and boredom. She was so mad at her parents for moving her to this crazy place that she would barely speak to them and stayed in her little hole they called a bedroom.

School finally started in the fall and that gave Olive something to do. Olive and her mom were usually arguing over silly stuff, everyday. Shiloh said her jeans were too tight, or she couldn't talk to boys on the phone yet, because she was only thirteen, she was too young to be interested in boys that way. Shiloh was strict but still a very good mother, a loving mother. It was a trying time for both Olive and Shiloh. Despite the silly teenage mother/daughter conflicts they were close.

Shiloh was great at baking things and was very excited one day when she got hired to work at a local bakery. It meant she would be working two jobs but she hoped for full time with the bakery.

"Olive, how about letting me French braid your hair this morning?"
"Sure mom, that would be nice."

As Shiloh braided Olive's hair they talked about Shiloh starting her new job that morning, how Olive was doing in school, and her new friends. They had a really nice, normal morning, this particular morning. This hadn't been the normal thing in awhile and it was nice for both of them to be getting along. It was time for Olive to go out to the bus, so she stuck her head back in the bathroom where her mother sat curling her hair and told her,
"Mom I hope you have a good day on your new job."
"Thanks Olive, I hope your day at school is good too, I love you, Olive."
"I love you too mom." Olive kissed her mom on the head and went to school.

Sometime after lunch Olive felt her stomach churning, and almost went to the school nurse, to go home. She argued with herself because she knew her parents were both working and didn't want to bother either of them. Her dad didn't like missing work and might get angry with her, and she knew her mom had just started the new job that very day. She would just stick it out, but she really didn't feel good. It must have been that cafeteria food.

When Olive stepped off the bus that afternoon she was so looking forward to laying down, and seeing her mom, to see how her day had been at the new job and let her know she didn't feel good. Just as Olive sat down on the couch to wait for her mother there was a knock on the door. Olive looked out and saw the landlady and wondered what in the world could she want. The landlady told Olive that the squad had to be called for her mom. Her dad had gotten off of work early that day and when he arrived home so had Olive's mom. They both had arrived home at the same time. Timing was crazy to say the least. Her dad usually didn't get off early.

Apparently Shiloh had a severe headache and told Olive's dad she was going to lay down a bit. At some point Olive's dad went to check on Shiloh and found her having a seizure. He had called the squad. The squad people had to go around back to get Shiloh because the hall wasn't wide enough for the stretcher. They had to take her out the back door because it was the easiest way to do it.

Olive sat there alone on the couch. The landlady offered to take Olive to her house but she had said she would be fine and would come up later if she needed anything. Olive sat there in shock wondering how her mom was doing, and just amazed with timing. When her dad and mom had come home from separate places that afternoon, it was the same time Olive had that sick feeling in her stomach at school. Some unknown, internal thing had been telling Olive something had been wrong.

Olive was remembering a conversation she'd overheard her mom telling her grandma one time. Shiloh had went in for surgery for a colostomy. During the surgery she recalled the Doctor screaming "Get back, get back, put the paddles on her. I'm not going to lose her." Shiloh told her mom that she was floating above her body, looking down and watching them work on her. She also remembers going towards a bright light and then boom she was back in her own body.

Shiloh had raised Olive not to believe in ghosts and all these strange happenings that people would sometimes talk about. She did believe in God's power and his angels, and the work an angel could do. Olive prayed for her mom. Finally Olive heard something from her dad. Her mom had to be flown to Charlottesville, Virginia. That was an hour away and Olive would have to stay with a couple in the trailer park. It was a preacher and his wife and two girls. It was a safe place until her dad could come back.

For two weeks Shiloh stayed in the hospital and had two major brain surgeries. Once when Olive went to see her mom in that two week period, she was allowed to go into the intensive care unit and see her. She was in a coma they said. She didn't look like mom anymore. She lay there with tubes running everywhere. Her head was nothing but white bandages. She was so pale and so thin. They said she weighed about eighty nine pounds. She never was that big anyways. She usually weighed around a hundred pounds when she did get around.

Olive went to her side and held her hand. Talking to her, telling her how much she loved her and missed her. How she just had to get better because dad couldn't cook as good as her. Olive's dad could cook but Olive was trying to lighten the air a little. One of the ICU nurses came by and told her not to expect too much out of her mom because she was in a coma and couldn't respond to her. Olive just stared at her mom until the nurse went away and then she whispered to her mom,

"Mom, I know you can hear me. She says you can't, but I overheard you tell grandma about the surgery where you could hear everyone around you. Just so you know mom, I love you."

Olive watched a tear slide down her mom's face and then when Olive told her to squeeze her hand if she could hear her, she did feel mom's hand twitch. She knew her mom heard her.

"Olive, I'm going to see your mom, are you going with me?" her father called from the other room.
"No dad, I'm going to stay here. I don't like going there. Can I stay here? I'll talk to friends on the phone or something?"
"Suit yourself, I'll be late. It's an hour both ways."
"Nah, I'll just stay here. Tell her I love her. She's still in coma, right?"
"Yes, she's still in coma. I'll talk to you when I get back then."

Olive told her father goodbye and shuffled off to talk to everyone on the phone. Olive messed around on the phone; talking to kids she'd met at school and at church. When her father arrived home late that night she got the information on her mom. Apparently it wasn't good. The Doctors couldn't get her out of the coma. They suggested unplugging her because if she did come out of it she would be a vegetable anyways. They didn't have much hope for her.

Olive shrugged it off in disbelief and went to bed. She lay there wide awake, staring at the ceiling in that tiny bedroom. She didn't believe her mom might die at all. Not after being told that the doctors wanted to kill Olive before she was born. Something special had happened then and it would again. She just knew it.

Olive was remembering a conversation her mother had with her before they moved. Olive had been home from school for some reason, enjoying the TV shows. It was close time for the news to come on but they broke in with a special on TV about the space shuttle getting ready for lift off, it even had a teacher on board, that would be exciting. They only had two TV channels in West Virginia and both of them were tuned into this. No cable where she was from. They couldn't afford one of those big satellite dishes that gave you lots of channels so they tuned into whatever was showing at the time.

All of a sudden to Olive's horror something went wrong, that space shuttle had problems and the thing blew up in front of her eyes. Her mom had come running in from the kitchen to see what had happened. Olive asked question after question to her mother. Olive couldn't imagine losing somebody like that. She'd been very upset.

Her mother got into a deep conversation with her and tried to explain to Olive that bad things happen and sometimes people die. Sometime Olive would have to realize Shiloh herself wouldn't be there either. She wouldn't be around one day and would die too. Olive didn't believe her mom would ever die. She would always be there. She'd beat all her cancer surgeries and she would always be there for Olive.

For the rest of that night and into the next couple of days Olive continued to believe her mom would be home soon. She would watch the clock every night until she fell asleep. One night she could not bring her mind to slow down enough to sleep, 10:30 came then 11:30 came and the last time she remembered looking it was 11:45. She drifted off to sleep… Dreaming this scene:

Olive lay there in the bed looking into the tiny hall; she saw an ambulance orderly dressed in bright white from head to toe. He was pulling a stretcher by her door with a white sheet covering a body. The face of the body slowly arrived in the doorway and rolled its head towards Olive. It was Olive's mom.

"Olive I have to go, it's time for me to go now. I just wanted to say goodbye to you. I wanted you to know I love you, and you're going to be ok..... "

There was a second orderly at Shiloh's head, as they pushed Shiloh by the door he covered her head with the sheet as it went out of site. It was the brightest white she had ever seen, almost glowing. Olive sat bolt upright in bed the phone was ringing, bringing her back to reality, out of the dream and wide awake. She ran into the hall where the dream had happened, making her way to the living room where the phone was jingling on the stand.

"Hello" she mumbled into the receiver.
"Hello, this is Dr. Johnson at UVA Hospital, can I speak to your dad please.
"She's gone, isn't she?" Olive numbly said to the Dr.
"Honey, I think its best if I speak to your father."
Olive glanced at the clock, it was 12:15 AM, "He's asleep, he gets up early for work, I don't know if I should get him up, he might get mad if I wake him up. Can I help you?"

"Honey its about your mother, it would be best if I talk to him right now."
"Okay," Olive said. She didn't have to call loudly because she heard her dad making his way down the hall just then. "It's the hospital daddy, its about mom she handed him the phone and went back to her bed.

She sat on her bed with her back to the headboard, and her feet under her listening to her father talk. He asked questions and thanked them for trying and then he hung up. She heard silence for a long moment then she felt his presence at the door.

He came in and sat down beside her. She looked up at him and then pulled her close, they both cried for a few minutes, and then he whispered

"She's gone. They said she went peacefully sometime between 11:45pm and 12:10 am."

They talked very little, then he hugged her and went to his own room and left Olive to herself. She lay there with hot tears rolling down her face. Her heart was broke, her mother was gone. One thing haunted her thoughts, her dream.

- This is a prologue of Carla Pleasant's e-book titled: **Olive's Mess-age**
- Available from Author House Publishing
- Available on Amazon.com
- Used as a testimony with Carla Pleasant's permission Monday, August 13, 2018
- As per her e-mail

Contact info:

Carla Pleasants
Luray, Virginia

E-Mail: **carlapleasants@yahoo.com**

Facebook:
**https://www.facebook.com/profile.php?id=10001211895
1266**

Psalm 27:5 For in the day of trouble He will conceal me in His tabernacle; In the secret place of His tent He will hide me; He will lift me up on a rock.

CHAPTER 10

FALLON HALE

My testimony is one of overcoming…

After praying about what to say I felt led of the Lord to write about my testimony of the goodness of God and healing with a couple encounters I've had with the Lord. The Word of the Lord says in:

Revelation 12:11 "They overcame him by the blood of the Lamb and by the word of their testimony."

So here is my testimony since coming out of the womb I've been fighting to live, and I truly mean that. I remember my mom telling me,

"You were premature, had yellow jaundice and after they let you come out from the Nic-unit, I always had to take you to the doctor for something."

My earliest recollection of having to go to the hospital was when I was 4 or 5 and I was even hospitalized because of being dehydrated. Since that time up until I was 12, I was sick every other year on every holiday, on Thanksgiving having bronchitis; Christmas the stomach flu, and on Easter pneumonia. I remember when I was five I gave my heart to the Lord, while attending a church daycare. This is an important part of my testimony of how the Lord has been with me since a young age.

The Word of God says in Proverbs 22:6 "Train up a child in the way he should go, and when he is old he will not turn from it."

This verse has truly proven itself to be true as, for me in my years of growing up strayed. I remember when I was 12 I rededicated my life to Christ, it was on a Sunday at the Baptist Church in Marion, Virginia and the pastor at the time who was female made an altar call and I responded. I remember it like it was just yesterday, my grandmother was the choir director and playing the piano. The pastor prayed over me and she not knowing any of the symptoms I have had since birth of being sick, prayed healing on me after I accepted Christ in my life. From that moment on I did not get sick every other year on holidays.

Another time in which I did not know that I was having an encounter with the Lord was when I was in Europe, with my high school French class. We were in Paris, France and I remember every church I would go to I would see the people walking by or sitting down smoking pot, and then walk in to the church. The one church in particular I remember going to was the Sacre Coeur, in which people would come in to do their Hail Mary's after smoking outside of the church and I just sat there and wept uncontrollably. I remember asking one of my spiritual mentors about this several years later and he told me that he felt it was the Lord using me for intercession. After leaving from the cathedral I had a man come up to ask me if I knew the Lord.

I told him, "I did," then he left and asked one of the people who were in the group traveling with that same question and that same person was not able to give the same answer.

Coming back to the states, I was preparing for my senior year in which I thought I knew what I was suppose to do with my life (sing in Italian opera houses and travel the world). Little did I know that I had a glimpse of what my destiny consisted of and so I began the journey of graduating high school and going to college.

Even in going to college, the Lord had strategically ordained my footsteps even when I wanted to do other things, he arranged it to where I would only be accepted to a Christian college, that led me to continue my education in North Carolina which led me to the church in which I would receive the Baptism of the Holy Ghost, as well as learn and get my appetite for the things of the Spirit. I was 18 or 19 and I had just began going to a Pentecostal Church in Valdese, North Carolina, and the first encounter I had while just beginning at that church, I remember hearing the

Lord speak to me through the Word of God, and then confirming it two weeks after. This was the first time I had encountered the Spirit of the Lord in the form of prophecy. The Word of God says that the testimony of Jesus is the spirit of prophecy, in Revelation 19:10. There were several things I remember from this precious season in time of the Lord in which I took for granted. One time in particular I was sitting in a church service in which the pastor was teaching about the power of God and how he healed through the generals of the faith. This is what sparked a fire in me to learn more about healing and led to the experience I had in my own home during personal prayer time. During this time I was experiencing extreme back pain and had no clue about how to pray for healing but I had heard that I could be healed, so I laid my hands on my back where the pain was and I felt heat in my hand while I was praying for my back. After praying my back felt better. This was also during the time in which I was seeking more than salvation in the Lord.

   While salvation is the beginning it's not the end. Salvation is the greatest gift we can receive from the Lord.

Romans 10:9 states "That if you confess with your mouth, Jesus is Lord, and believe in your heart that God raised him from the dead, you will be saved."

It's that easy and the life he has for us is great and abundant, if we only follow his plan. As I said earlier while living in the western North Carolina area is where the Lord chose to keep me hidden so that he could teach me, and I could learn and grow in the basics and wet my whistle so to speak in the things of the spirit. I remember when I received the baptism of the Holy Ghost, and I truly believe that I received these gifts in a night vision, as I had dreamed about how I was going to receive the gift of

tongues two weeks before on February 14th when I
experienced the gift of tongues. Since receiving the baptism
of the Holy Ghost, in the evidence of speaking in tongues
I've seen and experienced several encounters.

After a three year season of learning things of the Lord, I
remember the Lord specifically speaking to me one day
about him wanting to move me. I at the time thought I was
going to be moving to Missouri, but plans failed and I
ended up moving back to Virginia, where I was born and
raised. Looking back on this I know that the Lord had his
hand and dealings in this. As I know if the Lord had given
me specific details about where I was moving to I would
have had the opposite direction as I did not want to move
back from where I was raised. I'm thankful that the Lord
knows best and doesn't show all his cards, as this is where I
would receive my next instructions in life as well as the
ministry which began to take place in my personal life.

In 2005 I moved back to Virginia and began to attend
Impact Marion where my spiritual parents are in Pastor's
Barry and Debra Taylor who have mentored me in the gift
of faith. This experience has been one of testing and trial,
but I have overcome the obstacles and I know that I would
not have been able to if I had not been taught and trained.
During this ten year plus season in my life I've seen signs,
wonders and miracles, (the things I prayed about in North
Carolina), I attended Bible College. I knew this would help
me find out what I was called to do; which leads me to the
next God moment in my life, going on a mission trip and
experiencing the power of God through praying for a blind
person.

It was August 2007 and a group of us left to go to Belize.
When most people think of Belize, you automatically think
white beaches, and crystal-clear blue waters. Well there is

another side of Belize, one of poverty, which makes the homeless in America look wealthy. I remember the first day we went out to invite people to the crusade, we were doing door to door ministry. I remember seeing a lady, who looked to have Parkinson disease, and we as a group prayed for her and we saw the power of God come upon her and the symptoms left her immediately. It says in the Word of God in:

Mark 16:15 "And He said to them, "Go into all the world and preach the gospel to every creature.

16 "He who believes and is baptized will be saved; but he who does not believe will be condemned.

17 "And these signs will follow those who believe: In My name they will cast out demons; they will speak with new tongues;

18 "They will take up serpents; and if they drink anything deadly, it will by no means hurt them; they will lay hands on the sick, and they will recover."

This is the great commission; the part I want to focus on is that they will place their hands on sick people and they will get well. The word clearly states that this is for anyone who believes, and since I'm a believer, and I believe what the word says, the Lord has to honor his word. Another miracle I saw through praying for someone was seeing the Lord heal a lady who was blind in one eye. The lady through an interpreter told us that she was blind in the right eye, so we did what the word says in Mark 16:18 and we saw the Lord make this lady well in her eye. This experience made a forever mark on my life knowing that the Lord truly still heals today.

The most recent personal healing testimony happened just within this past month. It was July 14th, 2018 and I was sitting on the bed; when I felt my heart go from flutter to beating so fast that my blood pressure cuff did not register my heart rate or my blood pressure. I manually checked my pulse rate after the cuff did not read it, and it was 176. I immediately called my sister who I knew would get in agreement with me in prayer. Once I called her and she prayed with me, my heart rate went down and the blood pressure cuff reading was 146/99 with a pulse rate of 117. That was high for someone who had just been sitting on the bed messaging a friend who had just had a heart attack. I also told the sister how I was just messaging a friend who just had had a heart attack. My sister told me that it's an attack from the enemy, and you don't need to go to the hospital. I went anyways because in the natural I have been dealing with blood pressure issues and just wanted to make sure everything was alright. I made it to the hospital and once I was taken back by the nurse practitioner, she ran labs and told me my troponin levels were slightly elevated and that it looked like I might have had possible heart damage.

I immediately reached out to my sister and other prayer partners who I knew would pray. The second and final test came back negative for heart damage. That was an immediate turn around from what the nurse practitioner had said. I give complete honor and glory to God, my healer and I am now on the journey to seeking a healing strategy from the Lord on how to get healthy.

Contact info:

Fallon Hale
Marion, Virginia

E-Mail: **fhale0003@gmail.com**

Facebook: **https://www.facebook.com/fallon.hale.7**

Psalm 51:6 Behold, thou desirest truth in the inward parts: and in the hidden part thou shalt make me to know wisdom

CHAPTER 11

EVANGELIST CHERRY DELANEY

I had given birth to a beautiful baby girl…

In January 2001, I tried to walk from my front door to my car parked on the drive way, which was only a short distance, and I found out I couldn't do so without being out of breath. I had given birth to a beautiful baby girl only a month before in December 2000, and during the last stages of the pregnancy, my blood pressure would go up and down, and I developed preeclampsia. Some weeks after my first episode of being out of breath, my other daughter, who was 2 at the time, was playing on the floor with her books, and I tried to tell her to pick up her books, and NO words came out! I knew what I wanted to say, but I tried to talk, and again no words would come out! I thought I had imagined what just took place, so I stepped out my back door to get some fresh air. And even though it had started to rain, I felt like it was raining inside my head! You know you watch a cartoon, and only one person gets rained on?

My husband was sleeping, and I did not want to disturb him, so I called a family friend and she offered to go with me to the ER. We got to the ER, and as I waited in the waiting room, I tried to talk to my friend, and again no words would come out. By the time they took me to the back, I was told that I had suffered a stroke on my left side which controls the speech. I found out that my heart was only pumping 10%, and this is what caused the stroke. By the time I was admitted, I had suffered several mini strokes, and I was immediately put on blood thinners, so I would not clot. I stayed in the hospital 10 days, and while there the doctors told me eventually I would need a heart transplant.

I remember talking on the phone with my oldest sister while in the hospital, and as I talked to her, I could hear myself talking, but did not understand my own words! My sister became so alarmed, she called our aunt who was a pastor (she is deceased now) and she came to the hospital and prayed the prayer of faith over me.

The Bible says if there is any sick among you, call for the

Elders of the church, and let them pray over him, anointing him with oil in the name of the Lord. (James 5:16)

Over the course of time, because my heart was so weak, I began to fill up with fluid. I lost my appetite; I only had a craving for watermelon, which was not good for me because watermelon is mostly all water. My body was already over weight with fluid because of my heart not pumping right. Then I only craved corn starch and would eat boxes and boxes of corn starch. I would hide the corn starch under my bed because I was so ashamed that I was eating it. I would only want to chew it and spit it out, but I had to have it. A nurse later told me it was good I never swallowed the corn starch. My body was literally starving to death! I lost so much weight! I went from a size 22 to a size 9 in a matter of months, I looked like death. I remember a cousin who came to visit with me; and as I came out of my room and walked down the hallway to see her, she said to me:

"When will it stop?"

She was meaning when will I stop losing so much weight? But I had no control over it. I was sent to Shand's Hospital 60 miles away from home for 2 weeks, alone (my husband had just started a new job) I was to be evaluated for a heart transplant. I remember the doctors taking 8 liters of fluid off my body, equal to 8, 2 liter bottles of soda. I was told to watch my fluid intake. They asked you questions to see where your mind set was. Since my weight loss was new to me, I did not like the way I looked. The doctors want you to be as small as possible so your heart does not have to work so hard to pump. But I made it known to the doctors that I was not happy with all this drastic weight loss, and the doctor said to me,

"IF YOU DON'T LOSE WEIGHT, YOU WILL BE DEAD IN A YEAR!"

I never forgot those words, because I knew God was going to prove him wrong! I had said to him that you didn't see me before, I lost almost 12 to 13 dress sizes, but I still was not small enough for him, and for that reason I wrote that on my chart that he did not think I would take care of the new transplanted organ. But I think it was because I did not have good insurance, as my husband just started a new job. But what he did not know was I was praying to the Lord to let me keep the heart He gave me! When I was released, my appetite had returned, I have gone through a stone being lodged in my liver also and my eyes and skin turning yellow, BUT GOD!!!

It is almost 18 years (December 2018) since that beautiful baby girl was born, and I still have the heart God gave me. Three years ago, I did get a pacemaker with urging from my husband and the wonderful Christian heart doctor I have now. Truthfully, I did not want the pacemaker, but the Lord even put me at ease about that!

I had a dream a few days before I was to get a pacemaker, and in the dream a man said these 4 men will help me perform the surgery, so I knew that Lord was saying its okay, I AM with you! I still believe one day soon, I shall visit my doctor's office, and he will say:

"I DON'T SEE WHAT I SAW BEFORE, YOUR HEART IS HEALED!"

Now, I will take you through a few things the Lord has shown me! I remember lying on my bed one day home alone, and suddenly I could not move! I felt a demonic

spirit pull me by my leg to the end of the bed! I looked up
to the ceiling and I said,

"Lord, where are you?"
I saw a Glory cloud of smoke above me! I looked to my
open door and saw 2 people, a man and a woman walking
arm in arm in overalls walking past my bedroom door!

One day when my girls were in elementary school, (I
wished I had written down the date) I came home after
dropping them off to school, and suddenly I got so sleepy!
Normally I do some house work, but I could not keep my
eyes open! I lay down and I was almost asleep, but not
deep, and I felt my spirit leaving my body!

*"I said Lord, if I'm dying I am going to call on your name,
so I said, JESUS, JESUS, JESUS" in my mind 3 times and
when I looked we were in hell! I felt no heat, but I looked
and saw the biggest pot of fire! It was huge! Therefore, the
Bible says that hell is enlarging itself daily! The pot of fire
had no end to it!*

*Isaiah 5:14 Therefore hell hath enlarged herself, and
opened her mouth without measure: and their glory, and
their multitude, and their pomp, and he that rejoiceth, shall
descend into it.*

Jesus was standing beside me but I did not see His face, I
saw Him from the neck down (although I did not even see
His neck) He wore a long white robe, and He stretched His
hand out, and I followed His hand, and saw people in the
back of the fire. And I remember thinking they looked like
they have been here for awhile because they were grey
ashen color, and then I saw 2 people in front of the fire, and
they were in color. They had just arrived there, the man had
on a long sleeved blue shirt with tie. I remember thinking

he looked like a business man, and the lady had on a yellow dress, and they both had their arms outstretched wanting to be pulled out. I didn't understand it then, but later I knew the Lord was showing me what my calling was. Therefore, I often post and preach against sin, cause just like Jesus, I don't want anyone to be lost or perish!

I remember once sitting at my desk in my room and having a vision of the empty lot across the street from my house catching on fire, and 2 weeks later it did! The Lord has done amazing things and shown me amazing things! I will continue to trust in the Lord!

Favorite Scriptures:

Psalm 27:1 The LORD is my light and my salvation; whom shall I fear? the LORD is the strength of my life; of whom shall I be afraid?

2 When the wicked, even mine enemies and my foes, came upon me to eat up my flesh, they stumbled and fell.

3 Though an host should encamp against me, my heart shall not fear: though war should rise against me, in this will I be confident.

4 One thing have I desired of the LORD, that will I seek after; that I may dwell in the house of the LORD all the days of my life, to behold the beauty of the LORD, and to enquire in his temple.

5 For in the time of trouble he shall hide me in his pavilion: in the secret of his tabernacle shall he hide me; he shall set me up upon a rock.

6 And now shall mine head be lifted up above mine enemies

round about me: therefore will I offer in his tabernacle sacrifices of joy; I will sing, yea, I will sing praises unto the LORD.

7 Hear, O LORD, *when I cry with my voice: have mercy also upon me, and answer me*

8 When thou saidst, Seek ye my face; my heart said unto thee, Thy face, LORD, *will I seek.*

9 Hide not thy face far from me; put not thy servant away in anger: thou hast been my help; leave me not, neither forsake me, O God of my salvation.

10 When my father and my mother forsake me, then the LORD *will take me up.*

11 Teach me thy way, O LORD, *and lead me in a plain path, because of mine enemies.*

12 Deliver me not over unto the will of mine enemies: for false witnesses are risen up against me, and such as breathe out cruelty.

13 I had fainted, unless I had believed to see the goodness of the LORD *in the land of the living.*

14 Wait on the LORD: *be of good courage, and he shall strengthen thine heart: wait, I say, on the* LORD.

1 Corinthians 1:18 For the preaching of the cross is to them that perish foolishness; but unto us which are saved it is the power of God.

2 Corinthians 2:15 For we are unto God a sweet savour of Christ, in them that are saved, and in them that perish:

Contact info:

Evangelist Cherry Delaney
Daytona Beach, Florida

E-Mail: **sweetcherry64@live.com**

Facebook: **https://www.facebook.com/cherryd2**

Isaiah 32:2 Each will be like a refuge from the wind. And a shelter from the storm, Like streams of water in a dry country, Like the shade of a huge rock in a parched land.

CHAPTER 12

SUSAN J PERRY

Searching: The Closet of Pain…

This title was one of my first efforts in writing after God took me through much poetry. I was writing poetry, I was singing poetry; I was praying poetry and finally I was worshiping God with poetry. A very good friend of mine who has since passed away and is with Jesus was reading my poetry one day because I was so excited to share with him about what the Lord was doing through me. His name was Angel and he was an angel to me, a good friend, he and his wife helped me through so much in my beginnings with the Lord Jesus Christ! They actually discipled me which in itself is pretty miraculous; I was in awe of God! As we all have been at one time or another…

Angel was reading my poetry and I clearly heard him say, "You know this poetry is your worship to the Lord!"

I didn't realize this at the time. He always encouraged me. I was like a little child, reborn and saved at the age of 46. I now know why God is said to be "long-suffering" because He waited and drew me for a very long time. I suffered a lot. Why did it take so long? I was blind in sin and I was searching; I was lost and could not find my way until one day desperation filled me and I cried out to God!

Revelation 21:4 And God shall wipe away all tears from their eyes; and there shall be no more death, neither sorrow, nor crying, neither shall there be any more pain: for the former things are passed away.

God took a hold of me one night in pain as I cried and cried and cried until I was empty, because my situation and my life was desperately broken. All that I had or thought that I was, was broken by heartache, disappointment and discouragement and I was on my bed of affliction and I cried and called out to God:

"If you are real, help me!"

I cried until I thought my heart was going to burst or come out of my chest. I heard nothing. I had not moved anything or anyone. No help came or so I thought. I was nobody and nobody wanted me! I spent two nights like this going from weeping to sobbing back to crying like a wounded animal quietly drawing breath after crazy breath, it was a most difficult time. Even remembering it today, it's hurtful somewhat but I know it may help someone else. I have been healed in most of my memories. Our testimony is a resource from which God uses to help many and then many also read books to get some healing from what they have suffered. Yes there is help! Jesus Christ is our Savior and our very present help in the time of trouble.

Psalm 46:1 God is our refuge and strength, a very present help in trouble.

If you are in sin, trouble will follow you everywhere, you cannot hide from it. This book is about hidden things and hidden lives in the cleft of the rocks. And I had a lot of hidden pain although at the time I was unaware. Jesus died on the cross for me too and the sin I carried. It was awful! I had to find some release somewhere, somehow! I was desperate!

A friend of mine from work kept inviting me to her church in Houston, Texas. I resisted at first, I was afraid of change, I was afraid of accountability. I did not know there was a Savior who could change my life without shame or recrimination. I had so much guilt about my life; I was as scarlet as the Bible says. I was full of a lot of bad things and it was not of God but to His glory, I finally yielded and pushed forward.

Acts 16:31And they said, Believe on the Lord Jesus Christ, and thou shalt be saved, and thy house.

God knew how to draw me and help me to go His direction. God begin to turn me like the rudder of a big ship.

Acts 27:40 And when they had taken up the anchors, they committed themselves unto the sea, and loosed the rudder bands, and hoisted up the mainsail to the wind, and made toward shore.

You know God is showing me a large ship, how slow they turn to go in a different direction. They can't turn quickly but it's a slow turn until the rudder pushing through the heavy waters of the sea can get that big thing turned around and righted. That's like us who need to come to the Lord or are in the process of coming, God doesn't flip us over or turn us quickly but He does push us gradually until we are positioned correctly headed for that righteous path He has set before us. He doesn't want to wreck us or frighten us but to gradually bring us around to the things of God. God is talking about ships here but comparing us to the turn we must do. Isn't He a loving Father? He is so kind and faithful! Now I have heard many say they were radically saved and radically delivered but I guess that wouldn't have worked for me. I longed for a tender loving Father and later we could get into the bigger more explosive side of God. I longed for love, I was hungry for love. I was starving for love.

That's how God drew me was by His love. It's a big love we have and I will never forget those early days nor forget to be thankful every day. He is so good and I can't begin to measure His love for us to come unto salvation and stay close to Him. His ways are not my ways nor are His thoughts my thoughts but His are so much higher. But I'm going there with Him to be alongside Jesus forevermore…

I came from a family that did not attend church and one day my Grandmother Mary Baker asked me to go with her. I always loved being with my grandma. She was so sweet. She and my grandfather came and picked me up one Sunday and a few Sundays after that. I don't remember how many exactly but I do remember it was lovely and that it was short lived. Kinda sad but no one else picked up that ball. My family began to die one by one early and in strange deaths. I've since been told it was a generational curse held against our family. It was just my brother and I, my mom and dad until finally my sister came in 1965. My mom and dad had lots of sisters and brothers but we were a small segment of those larger families. First it was my mom, cancer was discovered in her lymph nodes while pregnant with my sister and she would not have any operation until she gave birth to her. She died in 1966; a year later after my baby sister was born. Then my baby sister died at age 28 in the year of 1994. She drowned during an epileptic seizure in a shower. My brother hung himself in his garage at the age of 53 in 2006 after battling so much disease in his body and mind and in his wife's illness as well. He turned away from all of us in his sufferings.

Now this was a beautiful young family that so many looked at and admired but not one of us knew Jesus Christ as Lord and Savior. The devil tore us apart in so many ways! But God; my mom accepted Jesus on her sick bed, my sweet Grandma saw to that; my sister had received Jesus late in her short life and my brother I could never convince. But that is a long story that I will not talk about here in this testimony. I have talked about it before. I want you all to know that God promises to save our families if we serve Him. His promises are yes and amen and although we suffer a lot in these times, we have certain guarantees. Believe them; our God is true and righteous. He saved all of my family, every single last one of them. He showed me.

My dad went home in 2013 at the age of 84. He lived a long life and I got to really spend some quality time with him in his last days. He told me that he knew God had been with him this whole time as he lay in the hospital bed. He went home on my birthday and that was hard to bear. My dad was a good man, he never served Jesus that I know of but he did believe. We had talks from time to time. I knew he saw the Jesus in me. God showed me my gift on my birthday was to be my dad going to heaven. Even though it seemed sad on that day, I was grateful for this gift. My dad is no longer suffering and I will see them all again one day. We have since broken that generational curse off of my family line. The devil comes to steal, kill and destroy but Jesus says He has come to give life and life more abundantly. (John 10:10) I have received that from God for eternity.

All my childhood, teenage years and as I grew up I was hidden in the rocks; hidden in the caves of life because if I stepped out and somebody recognized me, trouble would come and know me once more. I hid I stayed away from more hurt and adversity. But it found me any way because I was a sinner. I made poor decisions and unwise choices and I kept on going no matter the bumps and bruises. I was a healthy strong girl not often plagued by illness or sickness. But what they may call unlucky, I was. Now knowing God I say that we are blessed but in those days passed, it was different. I counted on luck not knowing God as I do today. I had friends but I was always alone. I had boyfriends and yet I survived lonely even when I was in a crowded room which I usually avoided. I didn't like people nor did I trust them although I was often smiling on the outside, I was broken on the inside and I wouldn't let many get close. I did not want any one to know about that hurt deep on the inside. I guarded it closely. I held on to it! It was mine!

After my mom died I walked around school like a zombie, I didn't know or care what was going on around me. I just existed. I barely passed my school classes to graduate, I was so lost. I had lost my direction and all I could see was hurt and torment. I recently learned from a friend of those old days that as we became friends, her mom had me checked out. I guess her mom was friends with the school nurse and she told her to look out for me because I was a bad one. Imagine that, a young lost girl at age 14 who just lost her mother and now had lost her way, a person of authority would say those hurtful things instead of reaching out a helping hand. It must have been some 45 years or so later that I heard this. I was in such pain. I forgive her now but we must be careful what we say to others. It gets back. See how God made sure I heard that much later on in my years with Him. He makes all things new! How many people have spoken ill over your life? Let us train our tongues which give way to either helping or hurting another.

Revelation 21:5 And he that sat upon the throne said, Behold, I make all things new. And he said unto me, Write: for these words are true and faithful.

God did this for me, He saved me. Now He uses me. Oh it's been a very long way and not always easy but I give Him all the glory.

The title of my testimony:

Searching: The Closet of Pain

It takes me back to Houston, Texas after I'd been saved for awhile. My whole life was being broken down for God's purpose; I was on the potter's wheel going around and around and around. I was hungry literally and I didn't see the light at the end of the tunnel and a friend of mine brought me a bag of potatoes to sustain me. It fed me again and again and I began to understand the things of God better and better and more and more. People helped me, they brought me lunches; bought me lunches and their leftovers, and etc. as God supplied all my needs. It was really tough at times. I survived but I was not blessed yet. I asked my potato girlfriend, what is wrong with me? What is happening? I'm broke, I'm tithing, and I'm loving and serving God the best way I know how.

She said, "Sue have you got any unforgiveness in your heart?" "Hmm, I said, I don't think so but I'll pray about it."

I pondered her question. It pricked me deeply. I never thought about it before; All those that had hurt or took advantage of me over the years; I had put and left them in the deep recesses of somewhere in my being. I didn't know where. Where do you put people you have never forgiven? Is there a place for them? Deep in the heart of Texas, that's where I was and I needed to get all the past out of me!

Psalm 51:1 Have mercy upon me, O God, according to thy lovingkindness: according unto the multitude of thy tender mercies blot out my transgressions.

2 Wash me thoroughly from mine iniquity, and cleanse me from my sin.

3 For I acknowledge my transgressions: and my sin is ever before me.

4 Against thee, thee only, have I sinned, and done this evil in thy sight: that thou mightest be justified when thou speakest, and be clear when thou judgest.

5 Behold, I was shapen in iniquity; and in sin did my mother conceive me.

6 Behold, thou desirest truth in the inward parts: and in the hidden part thou shalt make me to know wisdom.

7 Purge me with hyssop, and I shall be clean: wash me, and I shall be whiter than snow.

8 Make me to hear joy and gladness; that the bones which thou hast broken may rejoice.

9 Hide thy face from my sins, and blot out all mine iniquities.

10 Create in me a clean heart, O God; and renew a right spirit within me.

11 Cast me not away from thy presence; and take not thy holy spirit from me.

12 Restore unto me the joy of thy salvation; and uphold me with thy free spirit.

13 Then will I teach transgressors thy ways; and sinners shall be converted unto thee.

14 Deliver me from bloodguiltiness, O God, thou God of my salvation: and my tongue shall sing aloud of thy righteousness.

15 O Lord, open thou my lips; and my mouth shall shew forth thy praise.

16 For thou desirest not sacrifice; else would I give it: thou delightest not in burnt offering.

*17 The sacrifices of God are a broken spirit: a broken and
a contrite heart, O God, thou wilt not despise.*

Amen.
*Create a clean heart in me oh God! Forgive those who you
need to forgive and forgive them all!*

When my friend left me with that question of
unforgiveness, I was in my apartment and I was rocked by
it. I am still rocked by it today as I bring it out of the
memory banks. This was probably somewhere after the
year 2000. I was saved in the fall of 1998. I do not know
the exact date but I got down on my knees at my bed and I
cried out to God and I had a God encounter, a visitation
from Heaven. He came, He touched my memory. He
brought the names to the forefront and I remembered and I
cried and I cried and I cried some more until I wept bitterly.
I lived in bitterness, I know that now. Name after name
flowed out of my mouth, the LORD was touching me, I say
yes to forgiveness and God touched me that day. I went
somewhere; it was as if I was in a fog of God's glory. I
couldn't see because my eyes were glued shut with tears
and hurt that I was not myself anymore. God poured me
out. I still remember that day with a vivid memory. Jesus
came to save me again from my hurt and shame and guilt as
forgiveness poured out like oil from my pores flooding my
very soul. I surrendered to God that day all my hurts, my
wounds and my burdens; I was poured out again and again.
I believe at the very end of it all I passed out because I was
out of it for awhile, exhausted. But I forgave. I didn't
know, I could have held onto it and went to hell with it. No
not me, I love Jesus way too much for that! God has
brought me a long way. Some times we say, I don't know
why I had to go through all of that? Why did I have to
suffer so much? Didn't Jesus suffer for us? How much did

He suffer? Maybe we will never know but isn't it a fruit of the spirit in long-suffering? We gotta go thru some things! Life is not always peaches and cream and sweet things but we must take the bitter with the sweet and embrace it.

Matthew 11:12 And from the days of John the Baptist until now the kingdom of heaven suffereth violence, and the violent take it by force.

This is the scripture that rose up in my spirit just now as I am led and while it's a journey, we must take it back; Forgiveness is divine. I was deceived into thinking I had forgiven everyone but I never verbalized it before God's throne until that day and He set me free. My heart was cleansed and I was brand new. I melt like wax before the Lord. I know God has spoken to me many times in my books to let everyone know,

"PLEASE FORGIVE ALL!"

It is urgent! Don't hold anything back, check your heart. Ask God to show you and He will always be there to guide you. Let not your heart be troubled! Jesus will return soon and we must get ready for the Bridegroom. Let us not be like the 5 foolish virgins but instead be like the 5 wise virgins, keep your oil fresh and clean and filled to the top. Your heart must be clean to know Jesus. He searches your heart regularly.

Matthew 6:14 For if ye forgive men their trespasses, your heavenly Father will also forgive you:

15 But if ye forgive not men their trespasses, neither will your Father forgive your trespasses. Amen.

There was this little girl who when misbehaved was set in a large dark scary room in a big wooden chair at the center of the room. I can hear her crying and crying until she sobs all alone until time passes. This frightened little girl was me. I was afraid of the dark and my mother knew this. I cried until I could not cry any more with the deep sobs of a wounded animal. I hated this tactic. I often felt wounded, misunderstood and punished without mercy. Some times I was a disappointment and I acted out to get attention and I attracted the wrong kind of attention. My mother was a disciplinarian extraordinaire. She knew how to stop me. Her childhood was miserable and now this overflowed onto me until this day I remember those days as harsh times.

Now when I am corrected if done harshly I retreat and avoid conflict at all costs. Even uttering a word may cause a slap to come across my face with verve. Today I avoid most of it all if I can, even with my own daughters. Do I need a psychiatrist, well maybe so? But today I have the Holy Spirit, my teacher and my counselor.

John 14:26 But the Helper, the Holy Spirit, whom the Father will send in My name, He will teach you all things, and bring to your remembrance all that I said to you.

One day I sought the Lord on a matter that disturbed me so much about others and the way they handled a matter so harshly and He spoke to me:

"You need your little girl healed."

Oh okay Lord let's do that. We don't want any words spoken here going unhealed or broken. God, please heal my broken places and to all those that read these words, heal them in Jesus mighty name! We all have memories; hurts and disappointments that have gone untouched on the inside of us. They have been forgotten and are deeply imbedded in your inner sanctum. Come on now right here…. Give it all up! Let's get healed and set completely free!

Psalm 107:20 He sent his word, and healed them, and delivered them from their destructions.

Thank You Lord you are so generous with your bride!

Today as I continue to write God gives me a revelation for my own life. This is July 16, 2018 while in my own Bible reading, sometimes scripture just jumps out at you and you realize it pertains to your own life. I had just begun the Book of Deuteronomy when I realized how lost I had formerly been in my old life before I got saved like the children of Israel who constantly backslid; murmured and complained and could not find their way around the mountain because they were too blind to see. Well isn't that the way we live before we accept Jesus into our lives? We keep going around that same old mountain of sin and in this darkness we cannot see or discern the mess we are in until we answer the door Jesus knocks upon.

Revelation 3:20 Behold, I stand at the door, and knock: if any man hear my voice, and open the door, I will come in to him, and will sup with him, and he with me.

I am sure that Jesus knocked many times on the door of my heart but I always felt so inadequate to answer it. Thank God I finally did in the Fall of 1998.

Until that door of salvation is opened and Jesus is allowed to come in we are likened to the stubborn, stiff-necked children of Israel because our lives are unfruitful until then. God opened my eyes to that this morning. I had not ever really thought I could be compared to any of them for the Israeli people are God's chosen people. But didn't He choose me too?

John 15:16 Ye have not chosen me, but I have chosen you, and ordained you, that ye should go and bring forth fruit, and that your fruit should remain: that whatsoever ye shall ask of the Father in my name, he may give it you.

But before I get too carried away with my own revelation, allow me to give you some scriptures that did the job for me; that which became rhema for me:

Deuteronomy 1:33 Who went in the way before you, to search you out a place to pitch your tents in, in fire by night, to show you by what way ye should go, and in a cloud by day.

Deuteronomy 2:3 Ye have compassed this mountain long enough turn ye northward.

Deuteronomy 2:7 For the Lord thy God hath blessed thee in all the works of thy hand; he knoweth thy walking through this great wilderness: these forty years the Lord thy God hath been with thee; thou hast lacked nothing.

Deuteronomy 2:13 Now rise up, said I, and get you over the brook Zered. And we went over the brook Zered.

Deuteronomy 2:25 This day will I begin to put the dread of thee and the fear of thee upon the nations that are under the whole heaven, who shall hear report of thee, and shall tremble, and be in anguish because of thee.

Isn't this just how God is with us before we get saved? He keeps us and sustains us while we get in trouble and wind up in a mess until we allow Him to pull us up out of the quagmire of sin to receive Him and He cleans us up and then gives to us power and authority over our enemies. Yes this certainly is the condensed version but it can be a long story to haul out and retell. But God is so good to reveal the truth to us morsel by morsel feeding us more and more.

I looked up on the internet the name of Zered, the brook Zered as in:

Deuteronomy 2:14 And the space in which we came from Kadeshbarnea, until we were come over the brook Zered, was thirty and eight years; until all the generation of the men of war were wasted out from among the host, as the LORD sware unto them.

We know God speaks names of things over our lives and over our walk with Him. The Bible says to crossover this brook and it had to be going from one place to another as I had this revelation today. Here it is:

Zered = Zared, luxuriance; willow bush, a brook or valley communicating with the Dead Sea near its southern extremity (Numbers 21:12; Deuteronomy 2:14). It is called the "brook of the willows" (Isaiah 15:7) and the "river of the wilderness" (Amos 6:14). It has been identified with the Wady el-Aksy.

Didn't the Israelites crossover from the wilderness into the Promised Land? Didn't we as sinners crossover from the darkness of sin into God's marvelous Light? We all needed help and God was the One to provide it, and He still does today.

You know I have read the Bible over and over many times; heard sermons and many, many words but not until today did the bell ring for me:

"Ding- dong, ding-dong! I got it!"

God is so good all the time, it says in Psalm 23: 1 *The LORD is my shepherd; I shall not want.*

2 He maketh me to lie down in green pastures: he leadeth me beside the still waters.

I can always depend on Him in every way! Thank You Lord today for what you've given me all my life. It is never insignificant to me. God has given me the promised land here on earth until we return to Him in Heaven and in salvation we come off of that mountain that we have traipsed around and around again and again until we became so weary, that we give it up and in our giving up, God was able to come in and work with us: save us; mold us and shape us until we were ready to cross the river into the promised land of God. It has been a glorious trip for me. Have I arrived? No way there is so much more to do and learn yet. At least I am beginning to get it. God's ways are becoming my ways. Am I still flesh and imperfect, sure but I am looking towards the prize and His name is Jesus. There can be no greater prize than His love and understanding by dying for us on the cross and returning to give us the Holy Spirit. Wow!! Can man do this for you? No way only God can be this generous with us. I thank God every day for saving me! I no longer have to search for that closet of pain because I am healed, forgiven, cleansed and set free. That door has been locked and sealed by the Holy Ghost! My life is in Christ Jesus and it is full of His surely, goodness and mercy... *Psalm 23:6*

Contact info:

Susan J Perry
Edgewater, Florida

E-Mail: **susiebqt987p@yahoo.com**

Facebook: **https://www.facebook.com/susan.j.perry.14**

Facebook Group Page:
https://www.facebook.com/groups/466028446922987/

Amazon.com: **https://www.amazon.com/s?url=search-alias%3Dstripbooks&field-keywords=Susan+J+Perry**

JESUS IS THE ONLY WAY

John 14:6 Jesus saith unto him, I am the way, the truth, and the life: no man cometh unto the Father, but by me.

GOD LOVES YOU!

If you don't know Jesus yet or made Him your Savior, then please let us help you here. If you have backed way off from God, stopped going to church or went back into the world. Please let us help you here. Jesus is the only way; He is the only solution; He is the only answer and if you think you have problems now, and then think again, please let us help you here. We ask you to please say a prayer with us and repeat it out loud so you will be saved. It is urgent because time is short. Thank you. Please pray:

"Dear Heavenly Father, I know that I am a sinner. Today I need a Savior. Jesus please come into my heart and forgive my sins. I ask you to cleanse me from all unrighteousness and teach me your ways. I want to start all brand new and I admit I need your help. I need your plan for my life and not man's. Thank You Lord for eternal life so I can be with you in Heaven. Amen."

Now please let us help you here: Get in a good Bible based church, turn from your old ways, read your Bible and fellowship with like minded people. Allow the Lord to help you by praying your concerns to Him daily. Learn to worship and praise Him regularly.

God bless you as you go, He will be with you always even until the end of the age.

AUTHOR'S CORNER

SUSAN J PERRY

The author Susan J Perry resides in Edgewater, Florida. She and her husband John both continue to publish books as the Holy Spirit leads. They are named: Simply This Publishing. All works point towards Jesus. She was born and raised in Schenectady, New York and he was raised in Racine, Wisconsin and together they are a team for Jesus growing exponentially as per their spiritual parents, Frank and Karen Sumrall who ordained them on November 20th, 2015 in Bristol, Virginia. They love working for the Lord! They love the Sumralls!

Susan is retired from the workplace and continues to focus on their ministry together. They have four children and five grandchildren being blended families. They enjoy traveling to see all of them as much as they can. Susan also speaks with women's church groups because God gave her a mandate to encourage and edify His women in these days ahead. Each journey, each book brings her that much closer to the Lord and her intimacy grows and abounds in those special times while writing. For now God keeps giving her new book titles and for the present she'll keep writing in the Holy Ghost while it is yet day...

John 9:4 "I must work the works of him that sent me, while it is day: the night cometh, when no man can work."

CURRENT BOOK TITLES:

The Samaritan Women Testifies

Simply This: The World's Greatest Message

Preach It Sister Girl!

ASK for WISDOM: The Safe Harbor of God

A Stone's Throw Away: A Woman Testifies

The Persistent Widow Testifies

The Woman Presenting the Alabaster Box Testifies

Great Holes in Your Pockets: Recovering All!

Hidden in the Cleft of the Rock: A Woman Testifies

by Susan J Perry

* These books are all available on Amazon.com

Some are also on Kindle Format as well

Galatians 6:9 And let us not be weary in well doing: for in due season we shall reap, if we faint not.

Made in the USA
Columbia, SC
16 October 2018